The Early Years
1903-1920

Georges Rouault

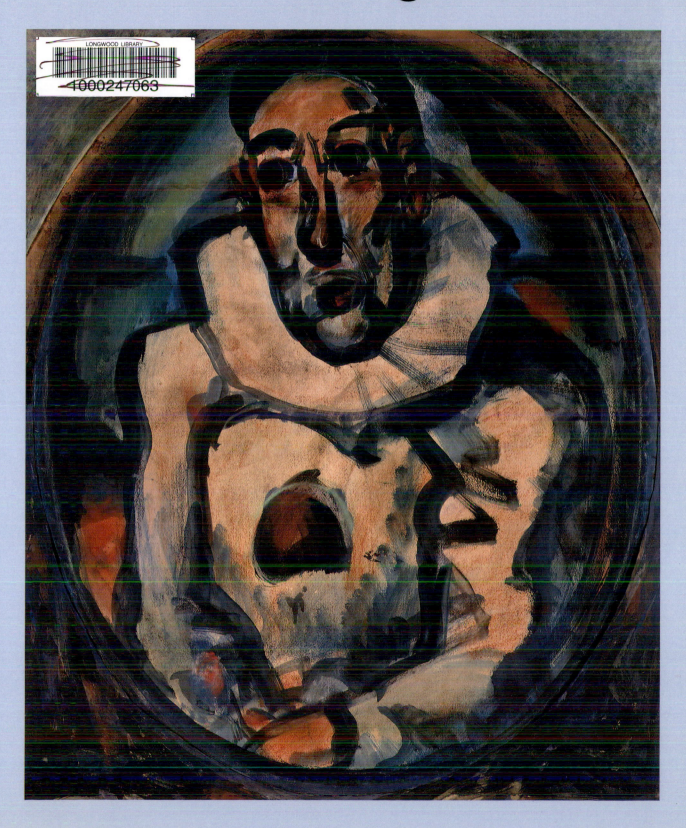

Georges Rouault

The Early Years 1903-1920

Royal Academy of Arts, London
11 March – 6 June 1993

Georges Rouault

The Early Years 1903-1920

Fabrice Hergott and Sarah Whitfield

Royal Academy of Arts, London, 1993

Catalogue published in association with Lund Humphries, London

First published in 1993 by the
Royal Academy of Arts in association with
Lund Humphries Publishers Ltd

on the occasion of the exhibition
'Georges Rouault: The Early Years 1903-1920'
Royal Academy of Arts, London
11 March – 6 June 1993

Exhibition Coordinator: Simonetta Fraquelli
Catalogue Coordinators: Simonetta Fraquelli, Jane Martineau
and Mary Anne Stevens
Exhibition Assistant: Charlotte Stirling
Catalogue Assistant: Sara Gordon
Photographic and Copyright Coordinator: Miranda Bennion

British Library Cataloguing in Publication Data
A catalogue record for this book is available from
the British Library

ISBN 0 85331 639 2

Designed by Alan Bartram
Made and printed in Great Britain by
BAS Printers Limited, Over Wallop, Hampshire

Sponsored by BMW 8 Series

in association with

Funded

With the support of the Cultural Service of
the French Embassy in London

Association Française d'Action Artistique

Ministère des Affaires Étrangères

COVER ILLUSTRATION
Self-portrait as Clown 1911 (Cat.70)

FRONTISPIECE
Self-portrait 1895 (Cat.2)

Contents

The exhibition was originally conceived and organised by the Musée national d'art moderne, Centre Georges Pompidou, Paris.

The exhibition organisers particularly wish to thank the following individuals for their advice and support.

Monique Barbier Mueller	Anne Lajoix
Philippe Bidaine	Réjane Laplanche
François Chapon	Yvonne Lehnherr
Anne Cherchève	Danielle Molinari
Liliane Decaen	Nicole Ouvrard
Bernard Dorival	Adam Repzka
Catherine Duruel	Cristina Scassellati
Jacques Faujour	Didier Schulmann
Siegfried Gohr	Nicholas Serota
Margrit Hahnloser-	Sarah Whitfield
Ingold	Anne-Marie Zucchelli

The Royal Academy of Arts is grateful to Her Majesty's Government for its help in agreeing to indemnify the exhibition under the National Heritage Act, 1980, and to the Museums and Galleries Commission for their help in arranging this indemnity.

List of Lenders

Basel, Öffentliche Kunstsammlung, Kunstmuseum
Bonn, Galerie Jochen Rackey
Collection of H. A. Gomès
Grenoble, Musée de Grenoble
Mrs John Hay Whitney
London, Tate Gallery
Lucerne, Galerie Rosengart
New York, The Museum of Modern Art
Paris, Ecole Nationale Supérieure des Beaux-Arts
Paris, Musée d'art moderne de la Ville de Paris
Paris, Musée national d'art moderne, Centre Georges Pompidou
Fondation G. Rouault
ex-Henri Simon Collection
Solothurn, Kunstmuseum
Tokyo, Idemitsu Museum of Arts
Tokyo, Galerie Yoshii
Valentin Collection – S.P.
Villeneuve d'Ascq, Musée d'art moderne
Zurich, Kunsthaus

and other lenders who wish to remain anonymous

Sponsors' Prefaces

Style and design are as synonymous with BMW as quality and technical excellence. For this reason, the visual arts feature strongly in our arts sponsorship programme.

BMW with its 8 Series Coupé is delighted to enter into this innovative partnership with the Royal Academy of Arts. The highly individual work of Georges Rouault will be displayed in the Sackler Galleries which have, appropriately, earned architectural awards for design.

To endorse its association with the visual arts, BMW has collaborated with contemporary artists since 1975 in the creation of the BMW Art Cars. This growing collection of unique vehicles tours internationally, illustrating that the world of technology and the world of art have found new common ground: the car.

TOM PURVES
Managing Director
BMW (GB) Ltd

BMW 8 Series is an award winner under the Business Sponsorship Incentive Scheme for its support of the Royal Academy Schools and the Royal Academy of Arts.

The Business Sponsorship Incentive Scheme, which is funded by the Government, and administered by ABSA (Association for Business Sponsorship of the Arts), is designed to increase the level of business sponsorship of the arts.

Harpers & Queen may be best known as an
enthusiastic celebrant of the luxury end of life, but
the magazine has always been actively involved in the
arts arena. The arts pages in *Harpers & Queen* have
a reputation for authority, wit and visual excellence,
and they are read avidly by enthusiasts of every art
form from opera and the big screen to all aspects of
the fine arts.

Harpers & Queen always champions the new and
exciting and it is particularly appropriate that the
magazine should be involved with this rare chance for
the British public to enjoy the early works of Georges
Rouault. His intense personal vision coupled with a
modern sense of compassion and social justice give
his work a poignant, contemporary appeal.

The exhibition being mounted in the new Sackler
Galleries is especially relevant. A dazzling
combination of light, space and technical innovation
designed by Sir Norman Foster, these galleries bridge
the gap between the traditional and the modern.
Harpers & Queen as an innovative, intelligent, multi-
faceted magazine, does the same.

JAMIE BILL
Publisher
Harpers & Queen

Foreword

Georges Rouault was a young man in Paris at the turn of the century. Apprenticed to a stained-glass manufacturer and later trained in the studio of the Symbolist painter Gustave Moreau, he also fell under the spell of the Catholic writers J.-K. Huysmans and Léon Bloy, and as a result nearly entered a monastic community. Such diverse influences produced a dynamic tension between subject and technique in his art which makes it exciting to study today. The verve with which Rouault put paint to paper, coupled with his expressive use of colour, is entirely his own.

This exhibition concentrates on the artist's early works painted between 1903 and 1920, an astonishing era in the history of European art; yet, surrounded by giants like Picasso, Matisse and Braque, Rouault holds his own with his remarkable powers of invention. Though we have paid him insufficient attention in this country until recently, his significance for the artist of today is obvious. The images he produced bear witness to the conscience of the twentieth century.

Our thanks are manifold. First, they go to the artist's family: his daughter Madame Isabelle Rouault who has so stalwartly defended the memory of her father and of his art. We thank her together with her sisters, Madame Geneviève Nouaille-Rouault and Madame Agnès Le Dantec, and her brother, Monsieur Michel Rouault. The exhibition was originally conceived and organised by the Musée national d'art moderne, Centre Georges Pompidou, in Paris; it then travelled to the Musée d'art et d'histoire, Fribourg. We are grateful to Dominique Bozo, President of the Centre Georges Pompidou, Germain Viatte, Director of Musée national d'art moderne and the Centre de Création Industrielle, and particularly to Fabrice Hergott, to whom credit must be given for conceiving the exhibition and giving it life. The Royal Academy owes a particular debt to Simonetta Fraquelli, who accomplished the task of reassembling the exhibition after its dispersal with her customary diligence. The Musée d'art moderne de la Ville de Paris, and many other museums and private collections throughout the world, have been exceptionally generous in supporting the exhibition with the loan of works of art.

It used to be said that no exhibition could take place without a sponsor. In these difficult times, when we can no longer take commercial sponsorship of the arts for granted, we are particularly indebted to BMW 8 Series and to *Harpers & Queen* for their generous support. We are delighted that the support we have received from BMW has taken the innovative form of an association with a particular brand, the BMW 8 Series, and also that this should have been acknowledged by an award from the Business Sponsorship Incentive Scheme.

SIR ROGER DE GREY KCVO
President, Royal Academy of Arts

'An outrageous lyricism'
Sarah Whitfield

Rouault was a strong, even an extreme, radical. It is hard to think of another prominent French painter of his generation so opposed to the fundamental tenets of modernism. His rebelliousness shows itself in his urge to disassociate himself from his own time, to turn his back on what he called 'this modern life on the streets', to claim that his real life lay 'in the age of cathedrals'. In preferring the past to the present, the old masters to the new, Rouault set himself apart from his peers. His stand against the motif was equally uncompromising. Most painters who worked directly from nature, he said, 'were tied to the motif like hanged men to the rope or guard dogs to the chain'. None of his contemporaries, not even those as independently minded as Matisse and Derain, felt the need to dismiss Impressionism so decisively. Matisse's own criticisms of Impressionism, his ultimate rejection of Signac and the theories of Neo-Impressionism, only came after he had thoroughly investigated their methods and theories. It was not in Rouault's nature to pit himself against the leading painters of the day or to measure himself against his contemporaries. If such an approach did not hold the same interest for him as it did for Matisse, it was not simply because of a difference in temperament.

When Matisse joined Gustave Moreau's class at the Ecole des Beaux-Arts in 1895 he was twenty-six and had only been painting for a few years. When Rouault arrived at the Ecole in 1890, although he was not yet twenty, he already had behind him five years of practical experience including an apprenticeship to a stained-glass maker and drawing classes at the Ecole des Arts Décoratifs. From an early age, therefore, Rouault possessed a range of experience and a mastery of technical skills that must have set him apart from his peers (perhaps it was also one of the reasons why he was such a favourite of Gustave Moreau's). This solid grounding (that was denied to Matisse, for one) surely gave Rouault the confidence to go his own way. His technical assurance may also account in part for the suddenness with which he developed a pictorial language all his own.

Rouault's account of the change in his work from the large sombre studio pieces he had painted under Moreau's guidance to the works that prepare the way for the violent lyricism of 1905-06 is told very simply: 'At that time I underwent a moral crisis of the most violent nature. I felt things that cannot be put into words. And I started to produce painting of an outrageous lyricism which everyone found most disconcerting'.[1] The 'moral crisis', which he suffered in 1902 at the age of thirty-one, had been slowly building up since the death of Gustave Moreau in 1898 and the departure of his parents to Algeria the same year to care for his recently widowed sister. His natural reclusiveness became an enforced loneliness, and he described his years in Paris between 1898 and 1902 as 'tragic'. The moral crisis, when it came, took the form of a physical breakdown so severe that he was convinced he was going to die. His recovery was followed by a period of convalescence at Evian, in the Haute-Savoie, from which he returned disgusted,

1. Georges Charensol, *Georges Rouault, l'homme et l'œuvre*, Paris, 1926, cited by Fabrice Hergott in *Rouault : Première période 1903-20*, Musée national d'art moderne, Centre Pompidou, February-May 1992, p.184

as he put it, with his sombre style of painting. Restored to health, he set about changing everything, his subject, his technique, his palette. The large compositions he had sent to the Salon des Artistes Français each year since Moreau's death, *Christ and the Disciples at Emmaus* (1899), *Orpheus* (1899), *Salome* (1900), *Christ and Judas* and *Orpheus and Eurydice* (1901), several of which were based on Moreau's own subjects, were replaced by works inspired by memories of childhood visits to travelling circuses, such as *Circus Performer* (1902, fig.a), or by figures of prostitutes suggested by the girls in the rue Rochechouart where Rouault now shared a modest studio. Canvas was replaced by paper, oils by watercolour, gouache, coloured inks, pastel, crayon – media of all sorts which he used either neat or with oil or petrol, sometimes mixing them together or applying one on top of another. The lightness and fluidity of these materials transformed Rouault's technique by giving him the liberty to invent and improvise on the paper. He describes the surge of creative activity that followed his illness with the excitement of someone describing a new and wholly unexpected beginning. Whether or not the moment of realisation was as sudden or as decisive as his words suggest hardly matters. In fact, the new style, as startling as it must have appeared in those works of 1902, needed time to develop. Rouault did not really hit his stride until 1904, but once he had, the euphoria of newness that carried the painting forward continued to do so over a remarkably long period. Remarkable, that is to say, in the context of Fauvism (which is the context of early Rouault), a style of painting which was equally euphoric but at the same time so fatally volatile that it burnt itself out within a few years. The outpouring of energy in Rouault's works outlived Fauvism by at least another six years.

Through his friendship with Matisse and Marquet, Rouault participated in the exhibition that gave Fauvism its name. In 1902, the three painters, all old students of Moreau, were involved in the setting up of a new exhibition space for contemporary art, the Salon d'Automne. It opened the following year, and in 1905 provided the arena for the most confident showing yet of works by Matisse, Marquet, Derain, Vlaminck, Manguin and Camoin who, thanks to the influence of Georges Desvallières, the Vice-President of the Salon d'Automne and the person in charge of the hanging committee, were able to exhibit as a group. Desvallières was also a good friend of Rouault's whose works he hung with his own in another room together with those of the Nabis painters and the subdued smoky canvases of Eugène Carrière. But although Rouault's works were hung apart from those painters soon to be dubbed 'Fauve', the critics decided otherwise, and treated him as one of their number. Thus, a reproduction of *Aunt Sallys* (1905, Pl.11, Cat.17) appeared on the same page of the picture magazine *L'Illustration* as Matisse's *Woman in a Hat* and *Open Window* and Derain's *Sails Drying* (fig.b). The fact that it looks at home there is not just because the

fig.a: *Circus Performer*, 1902.
Private Collection

fig.b: Page from
L'Illustration, 4 November
1905

vast difference in colour pitch between his painting and the others is disguised
by the black-and-white of the reproductions. It looks at home because it is a
painting about extemporisation. Rouault's touch has a freedom, an
unpredictability and a primitivism that match the spirit of the paintings Matisse
and Derain had brought back from Collioure in the late summer of 1905. The
practice of using mixed media adds to the improvisatory nature of the work —
the play between the mattness of gouache and the transparency of watercolour,
the watery blackness of *encre-de-chine*, the sudden dryness of a patch of pastel.
The swift notation may be more agitated, more precipitate than it is in Matisse
or Derain but like them Rouault turns painting into a script. 'I have a kind of
handwriting in painting', he was to tell André Suarès some years later.

fig.c: *The Theatre Box*, 1905.
Bührle Foundation, Zurich

A few months before the opening of the 1905 Salon d'Automne Rouault had
participated in a questionnaire on current trends in the visual arts conducted by
Charles Morice for the *Mercure de France*. In his replies he named the six artists
who interested him most: two old masters, Rembrandt and Goya ('I feel closer
to them than to all the other artists of our modern spirit') and four moderns,
Moreau, Rodin, Toulouse-Lautrec and Cézanne. Two painters who had figured
largely in the Fauve pantheon, Gauguin and Van Gogh, are conspicuously absent
(Gauguin, one of the artists Morice had specifically invited comments on, was
dimissed by Rouault more or less out of hand) but a third, Cézanne, was a hero
to Rouault as he was to the Fauves. The plenitude of form in Rouault's figures,
the way they swell out to fill the space around them, comes from observing
Cézanne's evasion of the contour. D. H. Lawrence, writing about what he called
'the mysterious *shiftiness*' of landscape, observed that this was a quality that
Cézanne got marvellously. It was precisely this quality of 'shiftiness' that
attracted Rouault. The use of transluscent lines of black, for example, around
the hat, arms, shoulders and shirt front of the male figure in *The Theatre Box*
1905 (Bührle Foundation, fig.c) frees the contour from a fixed position, allows it
to become slightly displaced and the form to expand. In *Girl at the Mirror* (1906,
Pl.13, Cat.30), a wide brushstroke of black which carries down the girl's back
and around her buttocks creates an outline which cradles the body in soft shadow.
In *Girls* of 1907 (Hermitage, St Petersburg, fig.d), the fullness of flesh is suggested
by the stroke of pink between the thighs of the standing nude, while the curve

fig.d: *Girls*, 1907. The State
Hermitage Museum, St
Petersburg

of the nude standing with her back to us at the top left is made with three or
four fat strokes of a black-blue. As in Cézanne's late watercolours of bathers it
is not only the transparency of the outline that gives the bodies their substance
but the multiplicity of strokes, the constant repositioning of a contour, the many
tiny adjustments demanded of the eye. Rouault's admiration for late Cézanne is
evident, too, in the bathers he painted on ceramic pots. These ample nudes, with
their slightly ruffled forms, merge as naturally into fresh, watery landscapes as
the bathers in Cézanne's small watercolours of the 1900s. One reason why
Cézanne's observation of form is so visible in the work of this period could be
that Rouault's skill, coupled with a remarkable facility with materials, gave him
the confidence to emulate the particularly demanding technique of Cézanne's late
works on paper. When Rouault attacked a work – and in these early paintings
that is exactly what he was doing – the watercolour, gouache and inks carried
with them a high level of risk. Mistakes in these media are not easily rectified.
The battered condition of *The Speaker* (1908-10, Cat.52), where pieces of the
paper have been cut out and replaced with others, together with the accidental
damage of cracks, peelings and paint loss, gives some idea of the gambles Rouault
was prepared to take.

Where Rouault was independent, not only of Fauvism but of the whole
Impressionist tradition, was in his choice of subject-matter. Even though *Aunt
Sallys* sits easily enough stylistically with Matisse's portrait of his wife on a page
of *L'Illustration*, its subject is of a different order. The ambiguity of the image
is strange and disturbing. The fairground game of pelting stuffed or painted
wooden figures with wooden balls is made more violent here by the suggestion
that the figures lined up in a row are no less real than the woman taking the
money. In the French version of these Aunt Sallys (the '*jeu de massacre*' of the
title), the figures traditionally represent a bridal group, with the bride seated in
the middle. Accordingly, Rouault places the bride at the centre of the composition
and makes her presence even more felt by means of a scrawl of electric blue pastel
around her hat which fixes her as the focal point of light. In creating figures that
are both alive and lifeless Rouault was following a tradition in painting that goes
back to the prefiguration of the dead Christ through the limp body of a sleeping
child. The example he may have had in mind, however, was nearer to hand. That
kind of ambivalence was a favourite theme of Goya's, a painter whom Rouault
particularly admired. When he painted *Aunt Sallys*, was he remembering the
image of Goya's *The Straw Manikin* (fig.e)? He would certainly have known it
in reproduction, and the infinite sadness of the tossed figure with its broken neck,
suspended above the circle of smiling faces, could hardly have failed to lodge in
his memory. The mixture of violence and pity, the sense of grief that is so much
a part of Goya's language, is also a part of Rouault's. Like Goya he depicts life
in terms of games and rituals, choosing the circus, the fairground, the brothel

and the courtroom as backgrounds against which his characters act out their parts. In *The Accused* (1907, Pl.20, Cat.40), an image of helplessness as extreme as that of *Aunt Sallys*, the body of the prisoner is sapped of energy and the arms hang loosely like a doll's. The clothes have a particular pathos, just as they have in Goya. The transparency of the white shirt, the suggestion of a frilled cuff, the brightness of the red cummerbund (the same red as the robes worn by the judges in *The Tribunal* (1909, Pl.22, Cat.56), are contrasted with the suffocating robes worn by the two officials flanking the prisoner and heighten his vulnerability. Goya's imagery can be seen too in *Girl at the Mirror*, a variation, perhaps, on the series of sketches (possibly intended for the *Caprichos* but never engraved) in which reflected images are thrown back at their owner in the shape of a caricature.

It was surely through Goya that Rouault found a subject-matter which lay outside the conventional iconography of Christian art but which allowed his profoundly religious nature to have full reign. The potential conflict between his commitment to painting and his commitment to the Catholic church may well have contributed to the strain that led to his collapse in 1902. In 1904, he was still troubled enough to write the following letter to the Abbé Mugnier (who had acted as confessor to Joris-Karl Huysmans, author of *A Rebours*, at the time of his conversion to Catholicism) : 'I love my art passionately, but there is more and more of a conflict between my art and religion ... It was even at the moment when I had the greatest need of religion to sustain me in my life and my art that the opinions and advice of very religious and very respectable Catholics sowed some confusion in me ... You will be able to understand what an artist is ... so completely engrossed in his art that he sees with a heavy heart that the conflict could well end in a deplorable renunciation of religion'.[2] Rouault may not have needed Goya's paintings to show him a way out of this impasse, but they provided a prime example of art as a form of moral protest, if such were needed.

In one sense Rouault's aims were not dissimilar from those of Matisse, or Derain or Vlaminck. In common with them, he identified art with expression. It was a word they all liked to use. When Rouault compiled his replies to the *Mercure de France* questionnaire in 1905, he ended by saying: 'Art, the art I aspire to, will be the most profound, the most complete, the most moving expression of what man feels when he finds himself face to face with himself and with humanity. Art should be a disinterested, passionate confession, the translation of the inner life, as it used to be in the old days in the hands of our admirable anonymous Frenchmen who sculpted the figures on the cathedrals'.[3] Compare that to the crucial paragraph of Matisse's 'Notes of a painter' published in *La Grande Revue* some three years later, in December 1908, which begins : 'What I am after, above all, is expression', and ends with the celebrated declaration : 'Expression, for me, does not reside in passions glowing in a human

2. Letter from Rouault to Abbé Mugnier cited in Hergott, op.cit., p.188

3. Hergott, op.cit., p.190

fig.e: Francisco Goya, *The Straw Manikin*, 1791-92. Museo del Prado, Madrid

face or manifested by violent movement. The entire arrangement of my picture is expressive: the place occupied by the figures, the empty spaces around them, the proportions, everything has its share'.

Rouault, like Matisse, was unable to distinguish between his feelings about life and his way of translating them into paint, which is why both painters give great weight to the word 'expression'. But, whereas Matisse assimilates the human presence into the overall composition, makes it subordinate, Rouault puts it in charge. In this sense it could be said of him that his means of expression are the exact opposite of Matisse's in that they do, most emphatically, 'reside in passions glowing in a human face'. The wretchedness that emanates from the colossal head of *The Accused*, or the furious indignation exploding from the eyes and the mouth of *The Speaker*, or the heavy bloated stare of *Monsieur X* (1911, Albright-Knox Art Gallery, Buffalo. Edmund Hayes Fund 1952), enforce the point that the key image in Rouault's art is the human head. Making the face the focal point of emotion is already apparent in the main figure in *Samson at the Mill* (1893, fig.f), the painting Rouault had submitted for the Prix de Rome in 1893, and the angle of the head of the blinded Samson, a slightly tilted three-quarter profile, was one that he was to make use of later, in *Clown with Accordion* (1906, Pl.17, Cat.28), for instance. The heads of Samson's tormentors also make a reappearance in *The Accused* (c.1908, Pl.23, Cat.51), where they are once again presented as grotesques (following medieval tradition the wrong-doer is presented as a caricature), but instead of the crude Bosch-like imitations of the early work, the faces are fashioned like carnival masks, and an air of masquerade introduces a note of grim levity. In some instances a small number of heads stand in for a crowd. This is the case with the four members of the jury visible in *The Tribunal* who, imprisoned in their box, their impassive faces laid out in rows, have an almost visible continuation outside the limits of the canvas. Similarly, the faces of the two clowns in *The Parade* (c.1907-10, Pl.16, Cat.47, fig.g) invade the foreground as though propelled forward by an invisible crowd. Then there is the face in the looking-glass which, like a mask, is a displaced face. In *Girl at the Mirror*, the reflected image is the double who looks back as though through another's eyes. The gaze, which has been transferred from the one looking to the one looked at, is directed more towards the spectator than the subject, making him a witness by drawing him into the painting, a conceit Rouault uses elsewhere. There is no avoiding the eye of the nude in *Girls* (c.1909, Pl.14, Cat.58) – it bores as mercilessly into ours as the eye of the clown in *The Parade* and obliges us to recognise that we too are these people's doubles. As Rouault told his friend, Edouard Schuré, 'I saw quite clearly that the "Clown" was me, he was us ... almost *all of us*'.[4]

Like Van Gogh, Ensor, Munch, Kirchner, Beckmann and Dix, all painters who have been labelled expressionist or Expressionist, Rouault belongs to the ranks

4. Ibid., p.185

fig.f: Georges Rouault,
Samson at the Mill, 1893.
Los Angeles County Museum,
Los Angeles

of the artists who have in them something of the preacher. They appeal to the
spectator by making him a witness to human frailty and suffering. The
Expressionist painter, or indeed the Expressionist writer, selects characters who
can be counted upon to elicit a powerful emotional response, hence the choice
of anonymous archetypes invariably picked from society's outcasts, such as 'the
whore', 'the drinker' and 'the accused'. In his own time Rouault was compared
to Toulouse-Lautrec, but the cabaret artistes and prostitutes painted by Lautrec
are incontestably realist because, like portraits, they depend on scrupulous
observation. They belong to their own time, unlike a prostitute painted by
Rouault, who, as Kenneth Clark pointed out, is closer to an '*objet de culte*', 'a
monstrous idol inspiring us with fear rather than pity'.[5] She is an invention,
sometimes based on memory it is true, but an invention none the less. As Rouault

5. Kenneth Clark, *The Nude*,
London, 1956, repr. 1985, p.334

explained: 'Nothing was calculated. I am no specialist in brothel women. So it wasn't the woman seen at the door whom I painted. That one and the others corresponded to the state of mind I was in.'[6] In fact, Lautrec's presence is visible in these works, but in the paint rather than in the subject-matter. Small areas of spattered pigment, in the fan held by the nude in *Odalisque* (1907, Pl.5, Cat.42), for instance, as well as in the background, suggest that Rouault may have been emulating the '*crachis*' technique that is such a feature of Lautrec's lithographs.

One way to define Rouault's expressionism is to define what it is not. It is not, for instance, nihilistic, and if that is a strain that runs through the work of many Expressionist writers and painters it is because they were more politically engaged than Rouault and closer, too, to the upheavals that brought about the catastrophe of World War I. His art is emphatically not one of negation. His response to the outbreak of war in 1914 was to embrace a more explicit Christian imagery, not to present the manifestations of violent death that are such a commonplace of Expressionism. His vision was one of affirmation, not Apocalypse. Nor is Rouault a self-absorbed artist. He shares little of the introspection of painters like Ernst Ludwig Kirchner who, for instance, when painting a self-portrait throws himself into a role, taking the part of *The Drinker* or *The Soldier*. If there is a measure of self-identification in Rouault's clowns it is no greater than our own. Where Rouault is closer to Expressionism is in his kinship with art outside his own time. Looking beyond their own cultural history was as important to the Fauves in Paris as it was to the young German artists of the Die Brücke group in Dresden and Der Blaue Reiter group in Munich, hence their common interest in tribal masks, children's drawings, naive painting and folk art. The eclecticism of the period leading up to World War I is vividly represented by the 144 illustrations embracing art of all periods and cultures published in *Der Blaue Reiter*, the collective almanac edited by Franz Marc and Wassily Kandinsky in 1912. Rouault's art, firmly rooted in European culture though it is, is not exempt from this spirit of discovery, or rediscovery. When Kenneth Clark compared Rouault's images of prostitutes to 'monstrous idols', the figures he had in mind were Mexican. And the comparison is surely just, for the massive, weighty bodies Rouault liked to paint belong to fierce and unappeasable spirits who exercise the same remote power as ancient fertility goddesses. Rouault's prostitutes, as Clark observed, are to be venerated rather than pitied.

The religious art of the past that Rouault responded to most overtly, of course, was not the anonymous artefacts of pagan cultures but the anonymous Christian sculpture of French Gothic cathedrals. The search for a transcendental image of mankind, which preoccupied artists in the decade before World War I and which led many of them to the work of anonymous African sculptors, led Rouault back to the anonymous Gothic sculptors of his own culture. While the forms of those medieval figures were very different from those of tribal art, their function was

6. Ibid., p.185

not; which is why Apollinaire, an avid collector, could describe the fetishes from Oceania and Guinea he kept in his apartment as 'Christs of another form and of another faith/Lesser Christs of obscure hopes'.[7]

It would be misleading to suggest that the stone figures of French Gothic sculpture determined Rouault's figurative style in the same way as the tribal masks in the Musée d'Ethnographie du Trocadéro in Paris determined Picasso's or the Oceanic wood carvings in the Zwinger in Dresden determined Kirchner's. Nevertheless, their impact, which is apparent more in the paint than in the image, travels through Rouault's work like a slow fuse. It is visible in *Girls*, where the head of the girl on the left is supported by a line of rough pink paint whose pitted surface suggests a texture of plaster or stone. But the effect of those stone sculptures is at its most obvious in the crusty surfaces of the later work, surfaces which are painstakingly worked up over long periods. From about 1912 onwards Rouault turned again to oil painting, translating the delicate surfaces of the earlier work, which were covered with rapid graffiti-like strokes, into heavily impastoed surfaces, crumbling with paint. The swift notation in the works realised between, roughly speaking, 1904 and 1912, gives way to a slower, more open-ended process in which the growth of a painting seems to matter more to Rouault than its completion. Once again, the example of Cézanne is apparent, but the early Cézanne, where the substance of the paint is so much in evidence. When the Paris dealer Ambroise Vollard bought 770 unfinished works from Rouault in 1917 he promised him that he would have 'the whole of his life' to finish them. The number of these works is surprising: if it represented his output from as far back as 1902 this would mean that he had left numerous works a year unfinished. It is as though Rouault was intent on giving his later work the same aged appearance as worn stone by building up over months or years rough, slab-like surfaces of paint. Some of these canvases, whether worked on over long periods, as so many of them were, or painted relatively quickly, have an abrasiveness that borders on the primitive. Matisse, for one, appreciated their grittiness. Pierre Courthion remembered seeing a reproduction of Rouault's *The Old King*, an oil of 1937 (Carnegie Institute, Pittsburgh), pinned to the wall of Matisse's apartment in Cimiez next to a colour reproduction of a Van Gogh. '"Look", Matisse said to him, "next to the Rouault, the Van Gogh looks like a painting from the eighteenth century"'.[8]

The Expressionist aim, according to the writer Iwan Goll, was to 'cram the largest possible content into the most acute and at the same time most simple form'. In quoting Goll in his book on Expressionism,[9] Roger Cardinal draws attention to 'the minute drawings of Wols or those "miniatures" scored by Webern where a vast orchestra is asked to condense all its resources into a performance lasting only a minute or so'. The sense of forces packed into a space they threaten to overwhelm is there in Rouault as it is in Matisse and as it had

7. Guillaume Apollinaire, 'Zone', *Alcools*, Paris, 1913

8. Pierre Courthion, *Georges Rouault*, London, 1978, p.116

9. Roger Cardinal, *Expressionism*, London, 1984, p.24

fig.g: Detail of *The Parade*, *c.*1907-10 (Pl.16, Cat.47)

been in Fauvism. Matisse achieved harmony not by imposing an order on the confusion of the real world but by quelling a turmoil of colour and design which he had induced in the first place. There is a similar sense of deliberate agitation in certain of Rouault's works, notably in the version of *The Parade* (Pl.16, Cat.47, fig.g). The purpose of the parade, which is to drum up an audience into a state of excited anticipation, is exemplified in one small detail. On top of the drum – the heaviest and most stable element in the picture – is a loosely knitted bundle of lines and colour patches. What it represents is not immediately apparent, but the amount of high-pitched energy massed within this small area of paint is like a microcosm of the energy stirred up in the surrounding space. And this is exactly what it turns out to be, for it represents the dancing shape of a small monkey dressed up as a miniature version of the clowns. In its depiction of movement, but above all in its expression of a crowd, of commotion and clamour, *The Parade* has an affinity with Futurist art. And Apollinaire's remark that Carlo Carrà, one of the foremost Futurist painters, could learn something from Rouault[10] focuses attention on the dynamism of these early works.

When Rouault described his style at this time as one of 'an outrageous lyricism' ('*un lyrisme outrageant*'), he made a telling choice of words. However informal, unpredictable, unrehearsed the marks on the paper or the canvas, however aggressive the subject, there is a restraining gentleness in the paint which allows a strong lyrical element to prevail. The gentleness is in the touch. *The Parade*, which is one of the most extreme of these early works in terms of style, that sets out to be both tough and slangy, is painted with the fluidity and deftness of a Cézanne watercolour. And this is perhaps the clue to Rouault's singularity, for, while he was only one of many painters of his time who chose to express themselves in violently expressive images, he was one of the very few who had the confidence to tread delicately.

10. Guillaume Apollinaire, *Le petit bleu*, 9 February 1912, cited in Hergott, op.cit., p. 204

The early Rouault
Fabrice Hergott

This exhibition covers the years from 1903, when Rouault painted his first paintings of prostitutes, to 1920, when he began to devote himself exclusively to book illustration, producing the cycles of engravings of which the *Miserere* was the most important. His artistic vision was formed between these two dates. From the time he left Gustave Moreau's studio in 1897, until 1903 his painting and his way of perceiving things had remained firmly under the influence of Moreau, his professor at the Ecole des Beaux-Arts in Paris. He exploited the work of those seventeen brilliant years for the rest of his life. On the pretext of working on engravings commissioned by Ambroise Vollard – who from 1917 was his sole dealer – he cut himself off from the world until 1939. The hundreds of paintings he started to work on during the short period covered by this exhibition constitute his visual legacy, both metaphorically and literally, and he spent the rest of his life reworking the same themes; he died leaving nearly a thousand unfinished works, which were donated by his family to the French Government after his death.

In 1903 Rouault was thirty-two years old. To his small circle of admirers he was neither the 'great Christian painter' nor the 'painter of human wretchedness' later portrayed (with sweeping over-simplification) in art history books. He was a mature artist, confident in his own ability, possessed of a classical education and of a thorough knowledge of the history of painting, which had been instilled in him by an art-loving grandfather and by his own efforts. He belonged to a group of Moreau's ex-students who remained loyal to their teacher. Moreau died in 1898, and at the turn of the century he was still held in high regard. Rouault, like his co-student Matisse, remained devoted to the memory of Moreau and grateful for his influence for the rest of his life. Whenever they met they would reminisce about his unparalleled ability to encourage and enlighten his students.

Rouault apparently got on better with Moreau than Matisse did, even though Moreau used to accuse Rouault light-heartedly of trying to simplify the art of painting. Rouault never questioned his teacher's instruction, and was later to recall in his writing the tremendous importance Moreau placed upon painting; Moreau's profound classicism did not, however, exclude a witty and broad-minded conception of what a painting could and should be. After Rouault's disappointment in failing to win the Prix de Rome in 1896, Moreau encouraged him to work independently. In 1897 Rouault painted the *Night Landscape* (Musée d'Orsay, Paris) in which two men are seen fighting in the foreground against a vast suburban landscape. In 1894 he had painted *Coriolanus in the House of Tullius* (Pl.1, Cat.1), one of his strangest canvases; from under the superficially academic veneer of the painting an animal tension emerges.

In his will, Moreau left his studio to the French Government as a museum and appointed Rouault its curator. The Musée Gustave Moreau, in the rue de la Rochefoucauld, was officially inaugurated in 1903. In reviews of exhibitions held there before World War I, critics and journalists often contrasted the official position of the young painter in charge of the museum with the excesses of his paintings. Rouault's attitude to Moreau was more than one just of respect: he defended his master's painting against the mockery of some of his friends who claimed that a knowledge of Greek mythology was all that was required for an understanding of his work. Rouault moved house frequently before giving up his curatorship in the early 1930s, but he always tried to be close to the rue de la Rochefoucauld. This was the period of his association with Degas, of his visits to Renoir and of his admiration of Cézanne.

As a young man Rouault was an ardent Catholic. His political inclinations were towards Christian socialism, somewhere between anarchy and Evangelicism. Léon Bloy, the writer and disciple of Jules Barbey d'Aurevilley, was the literary exponent of this trend at the turn of the century. Later Charles Péguy became Rouault's literary mentor, but he never ousted the violent and vituperative Bloy from his pre-eminent position. With other painters and writers, Rouault became a follower of the writer Joris-Karl Huysmans, a Roman Catholic convert and fervent supporter of Moreau (an important recommendation in the eyes of Rouault). Huysmans went to live near the Abbaye de LiguGé, hoping to set up a community of Catholic writers and artists. Rouault joined Huysmans, but a law banning societies put paid to the plan, and he returned to Paris where he frequented the studio of Degas, and admired the work of Forain, Rodin, Carrière and – most of all – Cézanne. The subjects and composition of his first paintings after 1903 reflect the influence of these artists, though the influence of Moreau is still paramount. From Degas come the decentralised compositions and the treatment of the female nude as a mere object; from Forain the dark irony of his drawings and paintings; inventiveness was derived from Rodin, light from Carrière – though Rouault soon came to realise that Carrière's light was only fog. The influence of Cézanne was of crucial importance – he had heard all about Cézanne from Emile Bernard, who had visited him. Colouristically and in the monumentality of the figures, Rouault's prostitutes and bathers recall Cézanne's second phase, but the violence of expression is very much like Cézanne's work dating from before 1870. The *Circus Performer* (fig.a, p.13), a small watercolour of 1902, dating from before his breakdown, is directly related to some of the prostitutes he later painted between 1905 and 1909. The shading on the face and upper body falls somewhere between the mannered *Christ Mourned by the Holy Women* and his later works.

After Moreau's death in 1898, Rouault suffered a deep spiritual crisis. When he emerged from it he went to Evian for a rest-cure. There he was so taken by the beauty of the brilliant snow-covered landscape that, as he admitted later, his artistic vision was completely changed. When he returned, the dark colours he had previously used had been purged (throughout his life his paintings always came out darker than he intended). The real world seemed to him to have speeded up, to have become a livelier and more dangerous place than it was before. He began painting translucent watercolours which seem to have been executed with an astonishing degree of violence: one is struck by the mix of curiosity and hatred, and the absence of any attempt to be decorative; later this was interpreted as compassion for the prostitutes and a denunciation of their profession. The paintings of Picasso's Blue Period were similarly influenced by Cézanne at this time. But Rouault is not so much of an expressionist as he might appear. His careful composition and intense chromatic harmony are strong enough to sustain the extraordinary harshness of his nudes and prostitutes.

Apart from some views painted from his studio near the boulevard de Clichy which he shared with Albert Marquet for a few months in 1906, Rouault seldom bothered with the surroundings of the people he painted. His figures stand very close to the picture frame, which is sometimes curved inwards to make the picture look smaller. His women resemble the Great Whore of the Apocalypse more than the merry or sad prostitutes described by Guy de Maupassant in his short story *Maison Tellier*. The world Rouault painted had nothing in common with everyday reality. He shows us the dark aspect of each individual lying behind the superficial mask of the brothel or of the circus. Thus, his clowns and horse-riders are not the characters from the Cirque Fernando, which Rouault must have seen as a child, but the faces of people he saw around him in the street. His judges, too, are promoted from the local assizes to the eternal tribunal of the Day of Judgement. He raises his subjects out of their context by using their social status as a pictorial element, but this is only a façade: the façade disappears to reveal a background in which individuality and common humanity merge. Each character has the uniform of his or her profession – the lumpy body of the prostitute or the judge's robes. The fancy dress, however, is surmounted by a head that bears the scars – the grimaces and wrinkles – of a lifetime. What the prostitutes share with the clowns and the judges is the great disparity that exists between the professional garb and the individual who wears it. Rouault treats the prostitute's physical nudity as a disguise, which he removes as he paints.

André Suarès, Rouault's friend and correspondent, acknowledged that his subjects were on a different plane from those of Toulouse-Lautrec, with whom he soon began to be compared. 'You interpret your clowns and simpletons as a lyric poet might interpret the horror and wretchedness of a landscape', he wrote.[1] In a letter to Suarès, Rouault states clearly what he feels distinguishes him from Toulouse-Lautrec: 'There is a strange and unexpected turnaround as far as I'm concerned. People whom I do not know say to me, without my asking, "It's stronger than Lautrec". Now, I'm no critic, but I shall try briefly to interpret what they mean. It is not a question of being more or less strong. I'm in a different domain, as you know – you have observed it and understood it better than anyone

1. G. Rouault, A. Suarès, *Correspondance*, Paris, 1960, p.151. Letter of 11 October, 1917

24

else. On his own ground, Lautrec is stronger than I am. I have the arrogance to think that my clowns and prostitutes inhabit the realms of poetry; he is a very skilled representational painter and a poster painter but, dare I say it, he is not so original a pioneer of form and colour as was thought at first, and he is already beginning to date. He seems extravagantly realistic, whereas my forms, my colours and subjects come from my imagination.'[2] For Rouault, painting is first and foremost a problem requiring a pictorial solution. He searches for combinations of tone, colour and form which will allow him to achieve a harmonious whole, the sum 'of the emotions I experience in the face of the natural world'.[3] His chief preoccupation was to find the physical means to express this.

Rouault's pictures of prostitutes are non-judgemental; his portraits of judges carry no moral overtones. Judges and prostitutes alike are shown in the exercise of their profession. In the paintings of Daumier or Degas the person looking at the painting can be identified with the observer shown in the painting. He is outside the work and sees it as it were through a frame-shaped keyhole. With Rouault this distancing is much less resolved. The onlooker is buttonholed and taken aside, and is able to extricate himself only with difficulty. Rouault's prostitutes are stripped naked for the eyes of one particular onlooker, rather than for a crowd of people. Each rapid brushstroke translates an emotion, and the interplay between the face, the mirror and the reflection in the mirror clearly implies a missing element, a very important one – the onlooker's gaze. The painting closes in around it like a trap. Other paintings of judges and defendants show this device even more plainly. Accusers and accused are presented together on the same vertical plane, like the bars over a window in a prison cell. Rouault's moral stance seems to be guided by the rules of poetic equivalence: the pictorial existence of the accused, the judge and the prostitute are a function of their emotional intensity. Rouault seems unclear as to whether they are the cause of the emotion, or whether they are distraught because of it. He sees both sides, not so much at the outset or at the climax, but somewhere in-between; it is the strength of the attraction or repulsion they exercise on his eye (and heart) that counts the most.

The ugliness that Rouault's contemporaries accused him of pursuing deliberately is not based on the observation of his subjects' individual idiosyncrasies, but on the observation of their relationships to one another. *Aunt Sallys* (Pl.11, Cat.17), reproduced across a double page in *L'Illustration* of October 1905, illustrates almost exactly the half-abandoned shooting range that Céline makes his character Ferdinand Bardamu discover in the Bois de Boulogne in his novel *Voyage au bout de la nuit*. 'A fake wedding party: in the front row metal figures of the bride with her bouquet, plus the cousin, the soldier and the red-faced groom. In the second row, more guests, looking as if they had already been slaughtered a few dozen times'.[4] Rouault exploits the ambivalence of the

2. Unpublished letter from G. Rouault to A. Suarès, 30 September 1917, lent to the author by Madame Isabelle Rouault

3. G. Rouault, A. Suarès, op.cit., p.86

4. L. F. Céline, *Le voyage au bout de la nuit*, Folio edition, Paris, 1981, p.79 (First edition, 1932)

scene in his painting. Are these metal figures or real people? Are the balls in the front row placed there for the spectators, or are they for the wedding-party to throw at the spectators as they file past? The glow of twilight permits a kind of Baudelairean confusion of identities. When the light changes, appearances change and the nature of everything is altered.

As Rouault's pictorial ideas developed he set about reworking the paintings in his studio. The layers of paint built up, causing the figures to lose their original delicacy and become increasingly hieratic. He thought with his paintbrush in his hand, and transferred his thoughts to the sheets of paper or card in front of him, or into the letters he wrote so incessantly. He may have inherited from Moreau his mistrust of the first attempt and his irrepressible urge to repaint; his enormous appetite for work sustained him in both. Meticulous, and sensitive to details that might have seemed unimportant to others, he reworked time after time everything he said, wrote or painted. Witnesses recall that his conversation was ironic and baroque. His letters are written carelessly, full of crossings-out, and often scribbled on telegram forms, without punctuation – often totally contradicted by another letter written immediately afterwards. His correspondence indicates his state of mind. Alert, self-aware to the point of self-mockery (he represented himself as a clown), he really was the 'peasant attached to the pictorial glebe' permitted by Nature (his painting) to rest only at night. Even in 1917, when he undertook the series of illustrations of *Réincarnations du Père Ubu* and the *Miserere* for Vollard, he would repeatedly work far into the night. Rouault loved work and frequently began paintings which he was utterly unable to finish. When he estimated that he needed two years for a piece of work, he would invariably need ten. When he needed to correct a patch of colour in a painting he would repaint the whole work, and then abandon it. He would start out with the firm intention of finishing rapidly, but he would linger and procrastinate, following up a host of new ideas.

In his letters to Suarès, Rouault often dwelt on the technical problems he encountered. His chief preoccupation was not the development of his painting as such, but the most appropriate means of achieving the end he had in view. All techniques were acceptable to him, and all interchangeable. He needed complete mastery of a technique in order to transcend it. More of an artist than a craftsman, he never attached great importance to skilled technique, although he must have been taught to work meticulously in Moreau's studio. He preferred to use readily available and easily manageable materials, and was in the habit of painting on medium-sized sheets of paper rather than canvas. He worked flat on a table, physically close to the painting in progress and able to inspect it from above. His interest lay principally in his material, and in giving it maximum form and colour; working flat on a table prevented his paint from dripping. In his earliest attempts at decorating ceramics, his subject-matter follows the shape of the pot closely. His letters hint at the importance he gave to such work, and it is unfortunate that only a small proportion of the many ceramics he made in Metthey's studio has survived. He consigned at least half of his watercolours to the flames, many of them finished works, as complete as his oil paintings. His production was so enormous that the conventional hierarchy of techniques signifies little in Rouault's case – he produced oil paintings, ink drawings, prints and ceramics. His own perception of the aims and objectives of his art was profoundly original and personal.

When Rouault read Léon Bloy's *La Femme pauvre* (and, as a result, became a friend of the writer in 1904) he not surprisingly felt a bond with the energy that pervaded Bloy's work. Bloy, who held a violent distaste for anything he considered 'bourgeois', castigated, and finally totally rejected, social masks or disguises; by masks he meant the external aspect of things as well as moral attitudes and language. He justified his dislike with reference to his own reading of the Gospels. Bloy's diaries make it clear why Rouault appreciated the man as well as the writer. His tantrums were those of a man who could veer precipitately between 'fury and humour'; the storm would stop as suddenly as it had started, 'as placidly as can be'.[5] Bloy produced the most sustained stream of vituperation and abuse ever known in French literature, relying for its vigour on his absolute certainty that all appearances are deceptive. Both Rouault and Bloy pay the closest attention to different types of reality. The writer's thesis is that 'no human being is able to say with any certainty what he or she is. No one knows why he has been born, nor what his actions, feelings or thoughts signify'.[6] These statements are not far removed from Rouault's famous question 'Who wears no disguise?', which he used as the title of a number of paintings, or from the letter written to Edouard Schuré in 1905: '... I don't know why at the end of a sunny day, when the first star appears in the sky, my heart is gripped and poetry pours from my subconscious ... The gypsy caravan parked on the road-side with the bony old horse cropping the thin grass; the old clown sitting in the corner of his wagon mending his striped, spangled costume: the juxtaposition of shining, sparkling things made to amuse with the infinite sadness of life – as it appears from a short distance. I began to build on all this. I saw clearly that the "clown" was myself, it was all of us (or almost all). The rich, spangled garment is given to us all to wear, and we are all clowns to a certain extent, we all wear "spangled garments", but if someone glimpses us unawares (as I glimpsed the old clown), oh! who can truthfully claim not to be moved to the very depths of his soul by enormous pity. My fault (if it is a fault, at any rate it causes me untold suffering) is *never to leave anyone their spangled garb*, be he king or emperor. It is the soul of the person standing in front of me that I want to see ... and the greater the person, the more extolled he is as a human being, the more I fear for the good of his soul'.[7] On 24 May 1904, one month after Léon Bloy's 'definitive

5. P. Léautaud, *Journal Littéraire*, vol.1, p.596, *Mercure de France*, Paris 1986

6. L. Bloy, quoted by J. L. Borgès, *Le miroir des énigmes*, *Enquêtes*, Paris, 1957, p.181

7. G. Rouault, *Sur l'art et sur la vie*, Paris, 1971, p.150. Letter to Edouard Schuré

annexation'[8] of Rouault, Bloy wrote in his diary: '"*Per speculum in enigmate*" (through a glass darkly), says St Paul. We see everything upside-down. When we believe that we are giving, we are receiving etc. "Well then", a dear soul said to me in considerable distress, "we are in heaven and God is suffering here on earth"'.[9] In a short passage originally published in 1921, which is permeated with the effects of long solitary hours spent in his studio, in painting and in self-enquiry, Rouault applies Bloy's thesis to artistic matters: 'The noblest subjects are diminished by an unworthy mind, and, conversely, modest and simple things can be raised up and glorified. A so-called "inferior" art may suddenly find its redeemer. The language of form and colour demands to be thoroughly mastered, and a lifetime of dedication is required, as well as devotion to the nurture of one's god-given talents. Life is spent groping humbly, devotedly, for the meaning of Nature and Humanity.'[10]

An artist's religious beliefs cannot be ignored. The artist's vision of the universe is formed by his beliefs, and refined by his musings on religion and by his use of religious themes. Rouault's painting can be appreciated by someone who is not an ardent Catholic, but it would be difficult to understand his work fully without some awareness of the metaphysical, of the connections between the visible and invisible worlds, and of how this might affect the relationship between the spectator and the object of his attention. An appreciation of Baudelaire or Verlaine is indicative of such a sensibility, a view that is reinforced by the fact that the two poets were made the subjects of his paintings. To Rouault, a portrait is like a landscape; the light around a head is no less intense than the light around a Breton landscape or a Nativity. On 2 October 1904, Bloy wrote to Rouault: '"What are you up to?" It would be easier to tell you what I am not up to ... I have wept so much that I am rich in tears. When you die, that's what you take with you: the tears that you have shed and the tears shed on your behalf, an inheritance of bliss and of horror. By the tears one has shed will one be judged, the Spirit of God being eternally "fond of water". A talented sculptor is just finishing a portrait bust of me and I said to him "don't forget the furrows, the gutters that run down my cheeks from my eyes"'.[11]

In his letters and essays, Rouault gives the impression of observing the development of his own painting from outside. When interpretation is called for, he quotes the circumstances of his birth (he was born during the Commune, in a bombing raid), or the areas of Paris in which he was brought up, as if his images and his reflections could be linked solely by his activity as a painter. His paintings are often hard to date, and indeed have no real time except in the painter's mind. Rouault was not given to speculation; he was an observer given to reminiscence. The urban landscape of his childhood furnishes the backgrounds of his *Vale of Toil and Suffering* (fig.h, Cat.67). He depicted the wretchedness of the poor districts of Paris; post-Commune Paris with its bombed houses awaiting repair

8. L. Bloy, in his *Journal, II, L'Invendable*, Paris, 1958, p.227

9. L. Bloy, op.cit., p.235

10. G. Rouault, op.cit., p.65

11. L. Bloy, op.cit., p.242

fig.h: *Vale of Toil and Suffering*, 1911 (Cat. 67)

– many still displaying the charm of the Second Empire – streets going up to Belleville with large cobbles covered in horse droppings. All these elements are painted in a hesitant, somewhat uncertain manner. Light, however, is far from uncertain, and early on makes its appearance as the principal motif.

Later he recalled his own astonishment at the watercolours and pictures that he produced following his artistic change of direction in 1903. In retrospect it became clear that the road that led to them led also to his landscapes. By 1910 his anxiety still had not been dispelled. His involvement in the creation of the Salon d'Automne in 1902 made him, for a few years, one of the most active promoters of modern painting, but gave him little confidence on his own account. Although he may have appeared as the most violent of all the painters exhibited in the famous Salon d'Automne of 1905, he was never a militant supporter of Fauvism. He studied his contemporaries' work but did not himself have much faith in movements, and was sceptical of 'isms'. His favourite expression was Poussin's 'Painting is a silent art'. His personal refrain, 'Form, colour, harmony' is the reverse of an artistic theory; it is an expression of longing that marks a permanent confrontation with nature – not nature as reproduced in the studio but nature as seen on the outskirts of towns.

Perspective disappears; depth is the depth of bodies and their attitudes. Those nudes with their arms in the air are situated in the middle of a landscape into which they fit with plant-like suppleness. His earliest paintings of prostitutes had permitted him to distance himself from the charm of Gustave Moreau. Cézanne guided his first steps. 'We all owe something to Cézanne', he said. Rouault's study of *Bathers* around 1910 (fig.i, Cat.62), influenced by Cézanne's paintings of the same theme, is less harsh than his earlier paintings of prostitutes in which he thought his 'brush with sin' was all too evident.

By this time Rouault's paintings already seemed to be in a completely different medium. Is it his very individual use of colour, or his absorption of both Cézanne's painting and the spirit of Moreau, that makes his work so unusual – without parallel except perhaps in certain Cubist works of art? In his isolation, Rouault invented his own version of modern art. His reflections on his work gathered on his pictures like a powerful dust. Some pictures were finished rapidly and remain successful sketches. Others were pursued much further and were not finished for years, even decades. Rouault may be the only exponent of a style of painting whose progress closely resembles a natural process of evolution. His new compositions provided a kind of material complement to the spiritual component of his earlier work. Here is 'the stain of sin' transformed into a thick, brightly coloured mud. Meanwhile the drawing – a few black lines inscribed beforehand on the sheet of paper – formed both the skeleton of the figures and the outer edge of their bodies. The black outlines used after 1910 are not the equivalent of the lead contours in the medieval stained-glass windows with which his paintings have

fig.i: *Bathers, c.* 1910 (Cat. 62)

been wrongly associated. The lines give structure to the forms rather than just surround them; they are like an external, translucent skeleton that allows an unexpected interior brightness to shine out. Even when he uses only indian ink, Rouault manages to suggest different depths of tone which almost materialise into colour. The sinuous contour of an arm or a back conveys a certain temperature, or a quivering silhouette. Dramatic intensity is implied by curves in the drawing, and the white spaces produce a suggestion of colour. Some of the early sketches that managed to escape Rouault's thirst for reworking over the years demonstrate that quite casual-seeming works can contain keen observation. His irony is more light-hearted, his curiosity less intense than it was with the prostitutes.

If Rouault's most important works produced between 1903 and 1920 are studied in chronological order, one is surprised less by his initial violence than by his efforts, once he had abandoned violence, to maintain the original level of intensity. During the pre-war period his work had become increasingly tied to reality. Then there was a subtle shift of emphasis; the realism of his paintings around 1905 gradually gave way to an idealisation of form. 'I was born with a *horror of ugliness*, or of material reality observed in too great detail.'[12] His technique then became more sober – a generous black line and little colour – but his subject-matter expanded. Yet, the profile of a prostitute, a black king, three female bathers, Christ on the Cross – all share the same structure. In 1910, Jacques Rivière was the first person to notice the change: 'The figure represented is not just a shape drawn flat on the page of a scrapbook. This figure has compacted areas, convex bits, sudden violent distortions and is as solid as a rock. Like a rooted tree it draws strength from the matter to which it is attached, and partakes of its massive structure'.[13]

Rouault's preference for solitude made him indifferent to the world around him. Though he viewed society in almost biblical terms – war, massacres, landscapes and exile all became subjects close to his heart – obviously these subjects could be related to contemporary life, but Rouault made no special effort to be understood by his contemporaries (although he wished that they would understand him). His idea of the role of the painter dates from the encounter with Gustave Moreau described in *Souvenirs intimes*. He was to spend the rest of his life drawing on memories, from the time of his birth under bombardment during the Commune to the time when the snow-clad landscape helped him to recover from the depression caused by the death of his teacher. The resulting style of painting was created without his having to step out of his immediate surroundings. His modernity does not seem contrived – it appears to have blossomed with no effort beyond the effort needed to translate his profound and accurate observation of life (and life fascinated and dazzled him) into paint. Recalling past times permitted him to look at life from a certain distance as if he were looking at its reflection in a mirror – the mirror also held up by his models.

12. G. Chabot, in conversation

13. J. Rivière, 'An Exhibition of Georges Rouault', *La Nouvelle Revue Française*, 1910, pp.49-51. *Etudes*, Paris, 1924, pp.52-55

1
Coriolanus in the House of Tullius
Coriolan dans la maison de Tullius
1894 (Cat. 1)

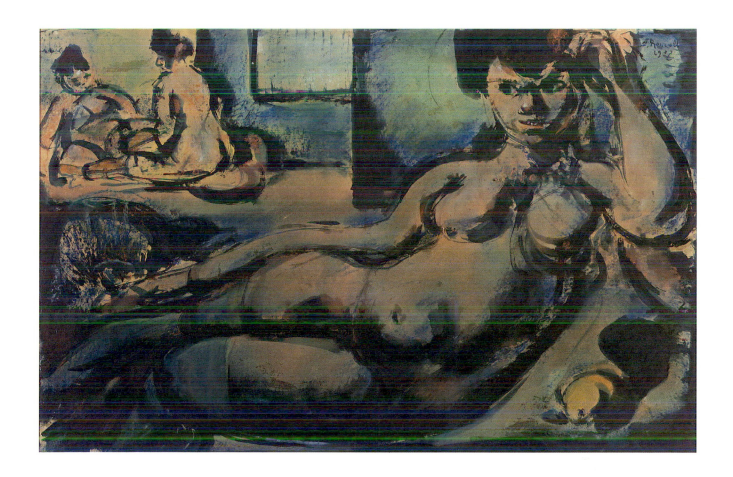

Versailles, The Fountain
Versailles, le jet d'eau
1905 (Cat. 11)

The Canal Boat
La Péniche
1909 (Cat. 53)

Dancer and Mr Loyal
Danseuse et Monsieur Loyal
1905 (Cat. 24)

The Circus (The Parade)
Cirque (La Parade)
1905 (Cat. 20)

Monsieur and Madame Poulot
Les Poulot
1905 (Cat. 9)

11
Aunt Sallys (The Wedding of Nini Patte)
Jeu de Massacre (La Noce à Nini Patte en l'air)
1905 (Cat. 17)

12
Girl
Fille
1906 (Cat. 31)

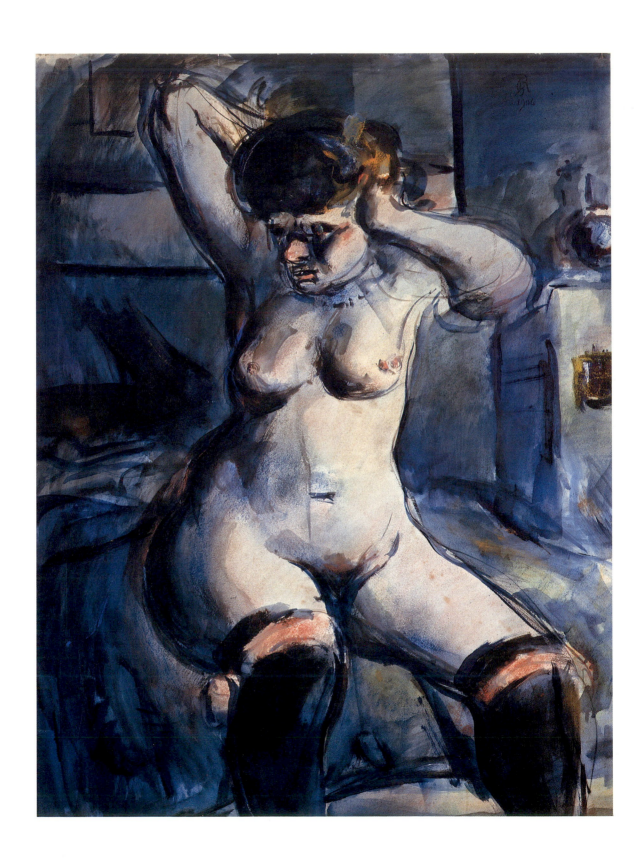

13
Girl at the Mirror
Fille au miroir
1906 (Cat. 30)

14
Girls
Filles
*c.*1909 (Cat. 58)

15
Girls
Filles
1905 (Cat. 16)

16
The Parade
Parade
*c.*1907-10 (Cat. 47)

17
Clown with Accordion (In the Theatre Box)
Le clown au bandonéon (A la loge)
1906 (Cat. 28)

18
Clown with Drum
Clown au tambour
c. 1903-07 (Cat. 5)

19
Clown with Monkey
Clown au singe
1905 (Cat. 23)

20

The Accused
L'Accusé
1907 (Cat. 40)

The Bride (Aunt Sallys)
La mariée (Têtes à massacre)
1907 (Cat. 44)

The Accused
L'Accusé
c. 1908 (Cat. 51)

24
Acrobat X
Acrobate X
1913 (Cat. 79)

25 (opposite)
Beastly Rosa
Rosa la Rosse
1913 (Cat. 77)

Rosa la Rosse.

26
Hortense
1910-19 (Cat. 63)

27 (opposite)
**Nude with Long Hair seen
from behind**
Nu de dos aux cheveux longs
1917 (Cat. 84)

53-3102

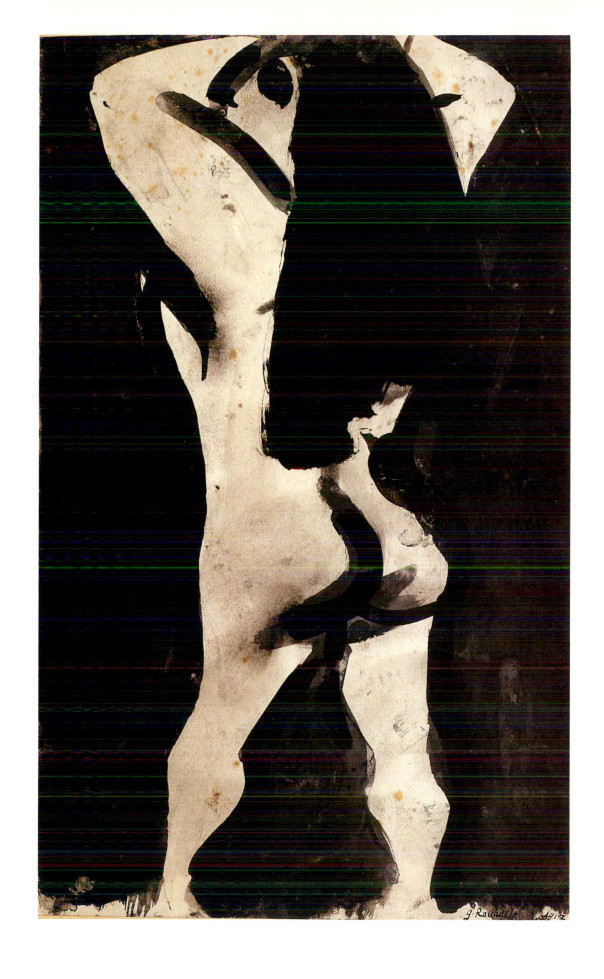

Project for Ubu Colon
Projet pour Ubu Colon
*c.*1917 (Cat. 86)

30
Christ Mocked
Christ aux Outrages
1904-09 (Cat. 8)

31 (opposite)
Christ Mocked
Christ aux Outrages
c. 1912 (Cat. 74)

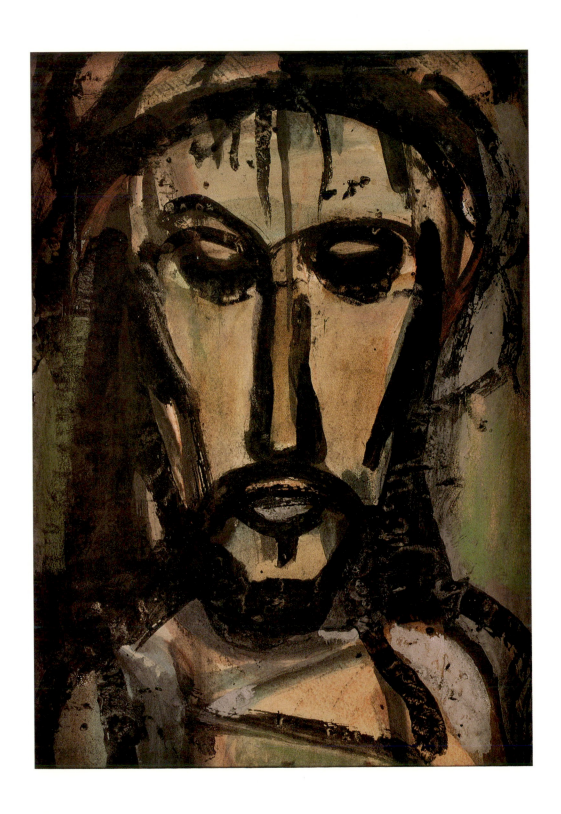

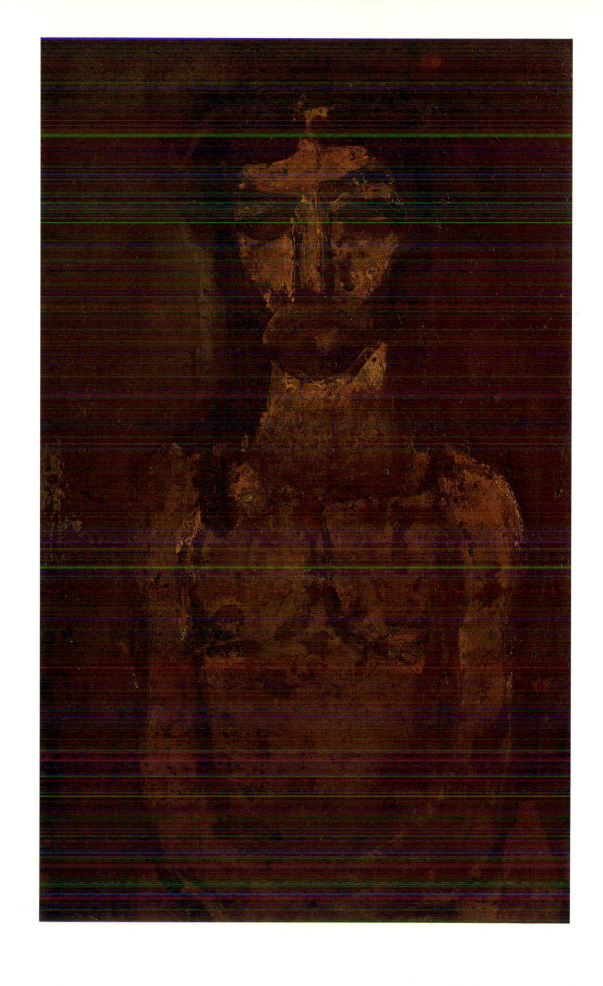

Christ on the Cross
Christ en Croix
c. 1920 (Cat. 88)

Chronology

1871-84

27 May 1871, birth of Georges Henri Rouault in the cellar of 51 rue de la Villette, Paris, during a bombardment of Paris by Government forces, when the Commune of Paris held the city.

25 June, he was baptised.

Rouault's father, Alexandre Rouault, a Breton, was a cabinet-maker who worked as a piano finisher and varnisher in the Pleyel piano factory; his mother, Marie-Louise Champdavoine, was a dressmaker. He had one older sister, Emilie. He spent his childhood in the working-class districts of Belleville and Montmartre.

His father, a follower of the liberal Catholic theologian Félicité de Lamennais, broke with the Church; Rouault initially attended a Protestant school but, after an unduly harsh punishment, he was transferred to a state school where he was a brilliant student.

1885

Rouault was apprenticed to a stained-glass maker and attended evening classes at the Ecole Nationale Supérieure des Arts Décoratifs. He was impressed by prints by Manet, Courbet, Daumier and Jean-Louis Forain, in the collection of his maternal grandfather, Alexandre Champdavoine.

1886

Rouault worked for Georges Hirsch, a restorer of stained-glass windows.

1890-91

Rouault's drawings caught the attention of Albert Besnard, a member of the Institut Français, who invited him to work on the windows of the Ecole de Pharmacie. Rouault declined, but was encouraged to enrol at the Ecole Nationale des Beaux-Arts. Through his friends, the Piot family, he met a Dominican priest, Père Vallée (1841-1927), who prepared him for First Communion.

3 December 1890, Rouault entered the class of Elie Delauney (1828-91) at the Ecole des Beaux-Arts; he made extensive use of the library and drew from plaster casts of antique sculpture.

5 September 1891, Delauney died and his class was taken over by the Symbolist painter, Gustave Moreau.

1892

13 March, Rouault entered Gustave Moreau's studio at the Ecole des Beaux-Arts, where the academic tradition was infused with an interest in contemporary developments in art.

1893

Rouault competed unsuccessfully for the Prix de Rome with his *Samson at the Mill*, (fig.f, p.18). At the end of the year, he received the annual studio prize for the most promising student.

1894

6 February, Rouault's *Coriolanus in the House of Tullius* (Pl.1, Cat.1) won him second place in the Prix Fortin d'Ivry for the best painted sketch.

July, his *Christ Among the Doctors* gained him the Prix Chenavard after his fellow-students protested against its initial award to one of Gérôme's students (Rouault's painting won a bronze medal in the Exposition Universelle of 1900).

1895

Rouault was commissioned by a collector and friend of Gustave Moreau, Léopold Goldschmidt, to paint two large canvases, *Stella matutina* and *Stella vespertina*. March, Henri Matisse enrolled in Moreau's studio.

Rouault again competed unsuccessfully for the Prix de Rome with *Christ Mourned by the Holy Women*; the painting was bought by the socialist deputy for Montmartre, Marcel Sembat.

Moreau advised Rouault to leave the Ecole des Beaux-Arts.

Rouault exhibited for the first time at the Salon des Artistes Français, under the name of Rouault-Champdavoine; his *Christ Among the Doctors* won an award.

1896

Rouault sent his *Christ Mourned by the Holy Women* to the Salon des Artistes Français. He spent the summer in the Vendée with the family of his friend and fellow-student at the Ecole des Beaux-Arts, Milcendeau.

1897

Painted *Le Chantier (Night Landscape)*.

fig.j: Georges Rouault, *Gustave Moreau*, Lithograph for *Souvenirs intimes*, Paris, 1926

1898

18 April, death of Gustave Moreau from cancer of the throat. Rouault was deeply upset by his death. Alone in Paris since his parents had gone to Algiers to be with his recently widowed sister Emilie, he began writing letters and poems, and decided to pursue an independent career, working in complete solitude.

1899

March, Rouault exhibited in the Salon des Artistes Français; he was considered to be Moreau's spiritual heir.

May, he completed pastel drawings of his parents and a large self-portrait in charcoal.

1900

Rouault entered a *Salomé* (one of Moreau's favourite subjects) for the Salon des Artistes Français. He met up again with Léon Lehmann, a fellow-student at the Ecole des Beaux-Arts, who was to remain Rouault's closest friend until his death. He painted landscapes in watercolour, and in pastel with wash or indian ink.

fig.k: The students at the Moreau Atelier
of the Ecole des Beaux-Arts, December
1897. Rouault Family Archives

fig.l: Léon Bloy. Rouault Family Archives

1901

Rouault submitted *Christ and Judas* and
Orpheus and Eurydice to the Salon des
Artistes Français.

Rouault, subscribing to J.-K. Huysman's
theory that artistic emotion was the
primary source of religious feeling,
believed that painting and religion were
closely linked. He and a few friends
decided to join Huysmans at the Abbaye
de Ligué in order to found an artists'
community. Legislation banning religious
associations prevented its realisation, and
Rouault returned to Paris at the end of
October. His friendship with Huysmans
continued.

Rouault became a regular visitor to
Ambroise Vollard's gallery at 6 rue Lafitte;
Vollard had been one of the first dealers
to show paintings by Cézanne and Gauguin.

1902

Gustave Moreau's bequest of his house,
14 rue de la Rochefoucault, Paris, and its
contents was accepted by the Government.
14 January 1903, Rouault was appointed
curator of the collection. Rouault came
into contact with Renoir this year, but did
not dare approach him.

Rouault founded the Salon d'Automne
with Matisse and Albert Marquet.

Rouault suffered a major breakdown,
and went to convalesce at Evian (Haute-
Savoie). On his return to Paris his painting

changed, probably following his discovery
of the natural world and landscape; he
also painted urban themes and people.

1903

Rouault spent a second holiday in the
Haute-Savoie at Annecy, where he stayed
with a relative of his art-school friend,
François Hermès.

In Paris, he met Edgar Degas.

1904

March, through a mutual friend, Auguste
Marguillier, Rouault first met the
conservative Catholic writer Léon Bloy
whose works Moreau had encouraged him
to read and whose intellectual
independence he already admired.

November, Rouault showed paintings of
prostitutes, clowns, acrobats and other
figures, together with some landscapes, at
the Salon d'Automne. Public reaction was
negative: he was jeered at and, with the
exceptions of Elie Faure and Louis
Vauxcelles, the critics, notably Léon Bloy,
reproached him for his dark colours.
Thereafter Rouault avoided discussing art
with Bloy, but he continued to admire him
and see him regularly.

1905

April, Rouault exhibited circus scenes and
prostitutes in the Salon des Indépendants.

June, at Bloy's house, he met Jacques
and Raïssa Maritain. Influenced by Bloy,
Jacques Maritain saw Christianity as a
source for the renewal of intellectual life;
he was the first person to appreciate
Rouault's new style.

November, at the Salon d'Automne
Rouault's *Aunt Sallys* (Pl.11, Cat 17),
hung beside works by Matisse, André
Derain, Henri Manguin, Louis Valtat,
Jean Puy and Maurice de Vlaminck in a
room dubbed the 'wild beasts' cage'
(*La cage aux fauves*). He also exhibited
Prostitutes, *Terpsichore* and *Monsieur
and Madame Poulot* (Pl.10, Cat.9), a
watercolour inspired by Bloy's novel *La
Femme pauvre*. (Bloy was indignant at his
book being illustrated in this way.)

1906

February, Rouault exhibited at the Galerie
Berthe Weil, in Paris.

March, exhibited at the Salon des
Indépendants. The theme of the dancer
made its appearance; his nudes were
described as having been painted with the
'disgust of a moralist'.

Rouault spent the summer near Avallon
in an abbey restored by Stéphane Piot,
brother of René Piot. He visited Vézelay
and returned there annually for several
years to come.

Rouault, accompanied by his friend

Paul Baignères, visited the potter André Metthey at Asnières, and began working with him. He met Ambroise Vollard at Metthey's studio.

Rouault's relationship with Henri Matisse grew closer as together they prepared the Salon d'Automne.

Rouault exhibited paintings and his first collection of ceramics.

1907

Rouault exhibited ceramics and watercolours at the Salon des Indépendants.

Granier, the deputy public prosecutor for the Seine region, who wrote art criticism under the pseudonym Aloysus Duravel, invited him to be a spectator at public hearings. During this period he painted his first pictures of judges, defendants and condemned men.

Trip to Belgium.

12 May, Huysmans died.

3 July, Ambroise Vollard suggested that Rouault make a series of ceramic pieces exclusively for him.

Rouault was a member of the jury for the Salon d'Automne that year and energetically defended Matisse's submissions: exhibited his first pictures of the law courts at this Salon.

1908

27 January, marriage of Georges Rouault and Marthe Le Sidaner, a pianist and the sister of the painter Henri Le Sidaner (1862-1939). She contributed towards household expenses up to the mid-1930s by giving piano lessons. They lived in the Musée Gustave Moreau, where their first daughter, Geneviève, was born in 1909.

Rouault showed his six *Decorative sketches* at the Salon des Indépendants and they caused a scandal, which was repeated at the Salon d'Automne. Only the *Mercure de France* gave a favourable review.

Jacques Rivière (1886-1925), André Lhote (1885-1962) and Henri Fournier (the writer Alain-Fournier, 1886-1914) were close friends and supporters of Rouault at this time. Rouault would take them on tours of the Louvre and they encouraged Gabriel Frizeau, the connoisseur from Bordeaux, collector, patron and friend of Odilon Redon, Paul Claudel, André Gide and Francis Jammes, to buy Rouault's work.

1909

Rouault exhibited two canvases in the Salon des Indépendants: *Judges* and *Girls*.

fig.m: Rouault with the Piot family, c.1907. Rouault Family Archives

He painted grotesque figures (motorists, lecturers, teachers) and his first working-class street scenes; also scenes for his *Exodus* and *Miserere*.

1910

The Rouault family moved to 51 rue Blanche, together with his parents.

February, Rouault contributed to an exhibition in Russia (Odessa, Kiev, Moscow, St Petersburg) and Warsaw with Matisse, Othon Friesz, Marquet, Le Fauconnier, Pierre Girieud, Kees Van Dongen, Derain, Marie Laurencin and Henri Rousseau.

21 February to 5 March, Rouault's first one-man exhibition at the Galerie Druet, 20 rue Royale, included 121 paintings, 8 drawings, 43 tin-glazed ceramic pieces and 10 glazed earthenware pots. The catalogue was edited by Jacques Rivière with a preface by Jacques Maritain (pseudonym Jacques Favelle) whom Rouault had introduced to Alain-Fournier and Rivière.

April, Rivière wrote an account of the exhibition in the *Nouvelle Revue Française*. Rouault's collectors included Stéphane Piot, Olivier Saincère, Roger Dutilleul, Henri Simon, the Hahnlosers, Marcel Semblat and his friend Georges Besson.

March, Rouault showed at the Salon des Indépendants (Apollinaire characterised his paintings as 'sinister', 'alarming caricatures of Gustave Moreau's works'), and in another group exhibition in Rome.

June, he showed in London.

September/October, he had several works exhibited in the Neue Künstler Vereinigung in Munich.

Further group exhibitions held at the Galerie Berthe Weil, at the Galerie Hessel, and Galerie Druet. At the Salon d'Automne he exhibited *Christ Among the Doctors*; it was bought by the State who deposited it with the Musée de Colmar where it was shown for the first time in October 1917.

October, birth of second daughter, Isabelle.

16 November, three articles by Rouault published in the *Mercure de France* in which he paid homage to Cézanne, Rodin and Carrière.

1911

March, Rouault showed ceramic designs in a group exhibition at the Galerie Druet and at the Salon des Indépendants where Apollinaire reversed his earlier, unfavourable, opinion.

16 July, Rouault embarked upon his long correspondence with the writer André Suarès. Suarès had already published major works that were critically acclaimed. (He was Gide's closest rival for the position of 'great French writer most popular with young people of the day'.)

September/October, Rouault invited to show at the Neue Künstler Vereinigung in Munich. He also exhibited in the Salon d'Automne. Some ceramics were included in the dining-room designed by André Marc.

Rouault had plans to publish a collection of his writings.

12-23 December, his second one-man exhibition was held at the Galerie Druet; it included 45 canvases, 11 monochrome works, 16 glazed earthenware pieces and some plates. Critical opinion was mixed.

1912

January, his third one-man exhibition at Galerie Druet: ceramics and glazed earthenware, paintings and drawings and watercolours gathered together in 'albums'.

June, the Rouault family moved to 36 rue de l'Orangerie, Versailles, where they were close neighbours of the Maritain family. After his father died Rouault began the indian ink drawings which were to become the *Miserere*.

August, birth of Michel, the Rouaults' third child.

Rouault published 'On the profession of painting' in *Gil Blas*. Collected notes written over a long period were subsequently published in 1926 as *Souvenirs intimes*.

September, Rouault submitted an article on Ingres to the *Mercure de France* declaring his admiration for the painter but also his suspicion over the recent enthusiasm for his work. He took part in a group exhibition in the Galerie Druet.

1913

Rouault submitted less work to the Salons. His letters to Suarès reveal a growing self-confidence.

He shared in group exhibitions at the Galerie Marseille (with Raoul Dufy, Dunoyer de Segonzac, Luc-Albert Moreau, André Lhote and others) and, in November, at the Galerie Bernheim-Jeune.

February-March, two of Rouault's paintings, a *Nude* and a *Parade*, and some drawings were included in the Armory Show, New York.

Vollard started negotiations to buy up the artist's studio which eventually happened in 1917.

1914

Joseph Florian, a Czech admirer of Léon Bloy and Rouault, printed the first colour reproductions of his work. For a long time Rouault considered these the best to have been printed.

The Rouault family moved to 15 Impasse des Gendarmes, Versailles.

He published 'Trois petits poèmes' in *Les Soirées de Paris*, a magazine edited by Guillaume Apollinaire.

August, war was declared, but Rouault's delicate health made him unfit for service.

1915

Rouault was haunted by the war in Europe.

December, his fourth and last child, Agnès, was born.

1916

January, Rouault ill and obliged to rest. He started work again in the spring. The American collector John Quinn bought a number of his *Grotesques*.

May, Rouault exhibited at Galerie Bernheim-Jeune.

June, the Rouault family moved to rue Blomet, Versailles.

After unsuccessful approaches to Forain and Derain for designs for book illustrations, Vollard commissioned a set

fig.n: Rouault with his wife Marthe and, from left to right, Isabelle, Michel and Geneviève.
Rouault Family Archives

from Rouault for his own *Réincarnations du Père Ubu*. Rouault accepted on condition that Vollard agree to publish his *Guerre et Miserere* and allow him to continue with his other painting.

1917

Vollard purchased Rouault's entire studio stock of 770 unfinished works promising to allow him to finish the paintings. 'You will have the rest of your life to finish them'. ('Vollard is never in a hurry, and perhaps I am not in enough of a hurry myself'; Rouault to Suarès.)

10 March, Dr Maurice Girardin, a passionate collector who had discovered Rouault at Galerie Bernheim in about 1910, bought four oil paintings and a watercolour at Galerie Druet.

From March onwards, Vollard declared he was 'enchanted' by Rouault's first sketches for *Ubu*.

Rouault suggested the purchase of premises in Saumur where his paintings could be safely stored. (The dealer accepted, providing that Rouault took care of everything himself, which he did free of charge.)

Vollard moved to Versailles.

3 November, death of Léon Bloy, aged 71.

1918

Rouault worked on *Ubu* and *Guerre et Miserere*.

He gradually abandoned gouache and watercolour in favour of oil painting.

1919

Constantly travelling between Paris, Versailles and Saumur, Rouault became exhausted by the preparation of the *Réincarnations du Père Ubu* and the *Miserere*.

1920

The Rouault family moved to 20 rue la Bruyère. Every morning Rouault worked at his *Miserere*, had lunch with Vollard and met other artists; in the afternoon he painted at Vollard's studio. Religious and circus themes now dominated his subject-matter, although *Miserere* (still under its provisional title *Guerre et Miserere*) demanded a considerable amount of his time.

November, Maurice Girardin opened a gallery, La Licorne, at 110 rue de la Boétie, exhibiting 50 canvases pre-dating Vollard's purchase of Rouault's studio. Rouault had not exhibited since 1916, and the press was generally favourable.

1921

The first monograph on Rouault was published in a series entitled *Les peintres français nouveaux*: it contained an introduction by Michel Puy and a selection of the painter's own writings.

1922

Small exhibition at the Galerie Barbazangues.

Rouault decorated a small plaque with *Clowns* for Henry Church.

1923

Rouault worked in solitude on his etchings and paintings.

December, Lhote published an article praising Rouault in *L'Amour de l'Art*.

1924

Vollard fitted out a studio for Rouault on the top floor of his own house, 28 rue Martignac.

15 May, Jacques Maritain published an important article about Rouault in *La Revue Universelle*.

March-April, the Flechtheim Gallery in Berlin showed works covering the period 1897-1924.

April-May, a retrospective exhibition of Rouault's early work at the Galerie Druet.

fig.o: Georges Rouault, *Face to Face with the Crocodile*, preparatory sketch for *Ubu Colon*, 1918.
Private Collection. Rouault Family Archives

fig.p: Georges Rouault, *Portrait of Ambroise Vollard*, 1925.
Private Collection. Rouault Family Archives

1925

Rouault presented his illustrations for the *Réincarnations du Père Ubu* at the Exposition des Arts Décoratifs – where they were received with general indifference.

He painted one of his most important works, *The Apprentice* (fig.q), a self-portrait.

He considered making a decorated fountain in homage to Cézanne at Aix-en-Provence, but the plan never materialised.

1926

Rouault published his *Souvenirs intimes*, a tribute to Gustave Moreau. In it, he also paid homage to Bloy, Huysmans, Baudelaire, Daumier, Cézanne, Renoir and Degas.

Georges Charensol's book on Rouault was published by the Editions des Quatre Chemins.

December, in the first and only edition of the magazine *Funambules*, Rouault reiterated his great admiration for Bloy.

1927-28

Rouault finished the 58 etchings for the *Miserere*. The work did not appear until 1948, published by Editions de l'Etoile Filante. He began to rework the *Réincarnations du Père Ubu*.

1929

He agreed (exceptionally) to work on the sets and costumes of Serge Diaghilev's ballet, *The Prodigal Son* (music by Serge Prokofiev and choreography by Balanchine). The ballet was staged at the Théâtre Sarah Bernhardt in Paris on 21, 29, 31 May and 4, 6, 12 June.

December, he paid a brief visit to the collector Fukushima at Montana-sur-Sierre (Valais, Switzerland). He burned his hands badly while disguised as Father Christmas to amuse the children.

Editions Porteret brought out Rouault's *Paysages légendaires*, poems accompanied by 6 lithographs and 50 drawings.

1930

The French Government refused to comply with the Musée du Luxembourg's request to purchase a painting by Rouault.

Rouault exhibitions held abroad: New York (Brummer Gallery), Chicago (Art Club), Munich (Galerie Neumann), and London (St George's Gallery).

Rouault worked on coloured etchings illustrating texts on the *Passion* and the *Circus* by André Suarès.

1931

Exhibitions in Paris (Galerie des Quatre Chemins), Brussels (Galerie Schwarzenberg), New York (Demotte Gallery) and Geneva (Musée de l'Athénée).

Illustrations for *Les Carnets de Gilbert* by Marcel Arland published by the Nouvelle Revue Française.

1932

Publication of *Réincarnations du Père Ubu* by Ambroise Vollard, with 22 etchings and 104 woodcuts by Rouault.

Vollard rejected the text written by André Suarès for *Circus* on the grounds that it might upset his clientele. Rouault offered one of his own poems, *Le Cirque de l'Etoile filante* (*Circus of the shooting star*).

Rouault's first tapestry, *Female Head*. Further tapestry designs commissioned by Mme Cuttoli were made at the Aubusson works (*The Wounded Clown* and *The Little Family*).

1933

The *Sacred Face* given by Mrs Chester Dale to the Musée du Luxembourg, the first of Rouault's works to figure in the collection of the future Musée national d'art moderne.

Rouault exhibition at the Pierre Matisse Gallery, New York.

Ubu presented at the Julien Levy Gallery, New York, and the Galerie Cardo, Paris.

1934-35

Rouault working on *Le Cirque de l'Etoile filante* and the *Passion*.

fig.q: Georges Rouault, *The Apprentice* (Self-portrait), 1925. Musée national d'art moderne, Centre Georges Pompidou, Paris

Exhibitions of works by Rouault at the Smith College Museum of Art, Northampton, at the Mayor Gallery, London, and at the Galerie Kaganovitch, Paris.

1936
Publication of *Le Cirque de l'Etoile filante* by Editions Vollard (17 etchings and 82 woodcuts).

1937
June to October, a selective retrospective exhibition held at the Petit Palais, Paris, as part of the Exposition Universelle, entitled 'Les Maîtres d'Art Indépendant', included 42 paintings by Rouault dating from 1905 onwards (20 on loan from Vollard). The public reacted with amazement and enthusiasm. At last, in the 66th year of his life, his work was beginning to be recognised.

October/November, the journal *La Renaissance* published an edition devoted to Rouault, including an important essay by Waldemar George.

Lionello Venturi began his study of Rouault, published in New York in 1940.

1938
Exhibition of Rouault's prints at the Museum of Modern Art, New York. A selection of his paintings shown in Basel with works by Vlaminck and Dufy.

1939
Publications of the *Passion* by Editions Vollard, with 17 coloured etchings and 82 woodcuts. Text by André Suarès.

22 July, death of Ambroise Vollard, following a car accident. Vollard's heirs sealed up Rouault's studio.

After the declaration of war, Rouault moved to Beaumont-sur-Sarthe.

1940-41
Moved to Golfe-Juan.

Exhibitions in Washington (Phillips Gallery), San Francisco (Museum of Modern Art) and Boston (Institute of Modern Art).

1942
April-May, exhibition in Paris, at the Galerie Louis-Carré, Rouault returned to Paris.

1943
Divertissement, a poem by Rouault, published by Editions Tériade.

August-October, edition of the journal *Le Point* devoted to Rouault.

1945
Major Rouault retrospective of 161 works at the Museum of Modern Art, New York.

Canon Devemy and Père Couturier commissioned Rouault to design five stained-glass windows for the Chapelle du Plateau d'Assy (Haute-Savoie). The windows were made by Hébert Stevens.

1946
April, joint exhibition of works by Rouault and Braque at the Tate Gallery, London.

Exhibition of 17 paintings by Rouault at the Galerie René Drouin, Paris.

1947
After many vicissitudes, Rouault won his lawsuit against the heirs of Ambroise Vollard over the legal ownership of his own works. The court decided that the painter was the owner of his own paintings 'provided that he has not given them away of his volition'. 800 unfinished canvases were returned to him, 119 had already been sold.

Publication by René Drouin of Rouault's book of aphorisms, collected by Abbé Maurice Morel and entitled *Stella vespertina*.

1948
April-June, retrospective exhibition (264 works) at the Kunsthaus, Zurich.

France sent 26 paintings and 12 prints by Rouault to the Venice Biennale.

Autumn, the *Miserere*, comprising 58 prints, finally published by Editions de l'Etoile Filante.

5 November, before witnesses, Rouault burnt 315 of the 700 unfinished paintings restored to him, knowing that, at 77 years old, he would never be able to finish them.

27 November to 21 December, *Miserere* on show for the first time, at the Galerie Odette des Garets, Paris, and warmly received.

Rouault travelled to Switzerland for the first time and to Italy.

He began a series of paintings based on a completely new range of colours – green, yellow and red.

1949

Rouault gave his permission to Dom Coquet for the execution of a series of enamels after his design at the Abbaye de Ligugé.

Travelled to Belgium and to Holland for the first time.

1951

6 June, exhibition to celebrate Rouault's 80th birthday organised by the Centre Catholique des Intellectuels Français at the Palais de Chaillot in Paris. First screening of Abbé Morel's film of the *Miserere*.

Rouault created Commander of the Legion of Honour.

1952

March-May, Rouault retrospective exhibitions at the Palais des Beaux-Arts, Brussels, and the Stedelijk Museum, Amsterdam.

July-October, retrospective at the Musée national d'art moderne, Paris.

1953

Rouault retrospective exhibitions at the Cleveland Museum of Art, the Museum of Modern Art, New York, the National Museum, Tokyo, and the Osaka Museum.

Named Commander of the Order of St Gregory the Great.

1954

April-June, Rouault retrospective at the Galleria d'arte moderna, Milan. The Girardin Collection exhibited at the Petit Palais, Paris. Named Corresponding Member of the Academy of St Luke, Rome.

1955

Rouault exhibition at the Jerusalem Museum.

1956

July-September, Rouault exhibition at the Musée Toulouse-Lautrec, Albi.

Physically exhausted, Rouault gave up painting at the end of the year.

1957

Reproduction of the *Holy Face* in tapestry, to hang above the altar of the Chapelle de Hem (Nord) (decorated by Manessier).

1958

13 February, death of Rouault at the age of 87.

17 February, by Government decree, he was given a state funeral at St-Germain-des-Prés.

1963

Gift to the Government by Mme Georges Rouault and her children of almost a thousand unfinished works by Rouault.

1966

Major exhibitions of Rouault's work organised by the Arts Council of Great Britain, shown at Edinburgh Festival (August-September) and Tate Gallery, London (October-November).

1971

May-September, centenary exhibition held at the Musée national d'art moderne, Paris. The review *XXe Siècle* published an issue in homage to Rouault, containing an article by Jacques Maritain. In it, he wrote: 'How is it that certain works of art seem to make us aware that we are receiving "an immortal wound" when we see them? Rouault's painting is pure painting, its sole concern the passionate exploration of the demands of the pictorial subject-matter, the sensitivity of the eye, the precise use of the most refined and appropriate technical means at its disposal. At the same time his art springs from the intimate depths of his soul, from the intensity of his interior vision, from his poetic intuition, confusedly embracing, in its emotion, the subjectivity of the painter and the mystery of the visible world. This is Rouault's great lesson to us'.

List of Works

1 (Plate 1)
Coriolanus in the House of Tullius
Coriolan dans la maison de Tullius
1894
oil
46 × 38 cm
Ecole Nationale Supérieure des Beaux-Arts, Paris

2 (frontispiece)
Self-portrait
Autoportrait
1895
charcoal and pencil
73 × 54 cm
Private Collection
Damaged by the occupying forces between 1940 and 1944

3
The Meal
Le Repas
1900
pastel on paper
27.6 × 28.3 cm
Tate Gallery, London. Presented by A. E. Anderson through the National Art Collections Fund, 1926

4 (Plate 3)
Bathers
Baigneuses
1903
watercolour
44 × 33 cm
Private Collection

5 (Plate 18)
Clown with Drum
Clown au tambour
c. 1903-07
watercolour and oil on paper
72 × 57 cm
Musée national d'art moderne, Centre Georges Pompidou, Paris. Gift of Mme Rouault and her Children.
One of the works which the artist kept for over thirty years: they acted as forms of self-criticism. He called them 'witness pieces'.

6
The Box Office of the Travelling Circus III
Caissières de cirque forain III
1904
oil
29 × 34.5 cm
Private Collection

7
Tragic Clown
Tête de clown tragique
c. 1904/5
watercolour, pastel and gouache on paper
37 × 26.5 cm
Kunsthaus Zurich. Dr Max Bangerter Bequest

8 (Plate 30)
Christ Mocked
Christ aux Outrages
1904-09
tempera and pastel
25 × 17 cm
Private Collection

9 (Plate 10)
Monsieur and Madame Poulot
Les Poulot
1905
watercolour
70 × 52 cm
Private Collection

10a
Girl at the Mirror
Fille au miroir
1905
recto (shown)
gouache and pastel
46 × 57.5 cm

10b
Standing Girl (seen from behind)
Fille debout (vue de dos)
1905
verso
watercolour and pastel
58 × 45.5 cm
Private Collection

11 (Plate 6)
Versailles, The Fountain
Versailles, le jet d'eau
1905
watercolour and pastel
67 × 53 cm
Private Collection

12
Olympia
1905
watercolour and pastel
27 × 43 cm
Collection of H. A. Gomès

13
Clown and Child (Father and Children)
Clown et enfant (Père et enfants)
1905
watercolour, gouache and oil on paper
16.5 × 11.9 cm
Private Collection

14
Mother and Child
Mère et enfant (La femme du clown)
1905
watercolour, gouache and oil on paper
16.5 × 11.9 cm
Private Collection

15
Circus Act
Numéro de cirque (La femme canon)
1905
watercolour, pastel, charcoal and ink
26 × 34.3 cm
The Museum of Modern Art, New York. Collection Joan and Lester Avnet

16 (Plate 15)
Girls
Filles
1905
black chalk, pastel on *papier collé* on card
23 × 23.5 cm

Musée national d'art moderne, Centre Georges Pompidou, Paris

17 (Plate 11)
Aunt Sallys (The Wedding of Nini Patte)
Jeu de massacre (La Noce à Nini Patte en l'air)
1905
watercolour, gouache and chinese ink on paper
52 × 66.30 cm
Musée national d'art moderne, Centre Georges Pompidou, Paris

18 (not exhibited)
At the Bal Tabarin (Dancing the Chahut)
A Tabarin (Le Chahut)
1905
watercolour and pastel
71 × 55 cm
Musée d'art moderne de la Ville de Paris

19
Christ and the Disciples
Christ et Disciples
1905
pastel, chinese ink and charcoal
14.5 × 15 cm
Musée d'art moderne de la Ville de Paris

20 (Plate 9)
The Circus (The Parade)
Cirque (La Parade)
1905
watercolour and pastel
33.5 × 27.8 cm
Musée d'art moderne de la Ville de Paris

21
The Fallen Eve (Nude at the Mirror)
Eve déchue (Nu au miroir)
1905
watercolour and pastel
26.4 × 21.5 cm
Musée d'art moderne de la Ville de Paris

22
Wrestler (The Parade)
Lutteur (La Parade)
1905
watercolour, chinese ink and
oil
22 × 12 cm
Musée d'art moderne de la
Ville de Paris

23 (Plate 19)
Clown with Monkey
Clown au singe
1905
watercolour, pastel and oil
40.2 × 25.7 cm
Galerie Rosengart, Lucerne

24 (Plate 8)
Dancer and Mr Loyal
Danseuse et Monsieur Loyal
1905
watercolour, pastel and
chinese ink
28 × 36.3 cm
Galerie Rosengart, Lucerne

25
Woman with Hat
Femme au chapeau
1905
watercolour
22 × 16.5 cm
Fondation G. Rouault

26
Circus Performer
Fille (La Saltimbanque)
1905/6
gouache on paper
41 × 23 cm
Musée de Grenoble

27
Seated Model
Le Modèle assis
1906
watercolour and thin wash
28 × 23 cm
Private Collection

28 (Plate 17)
**Clown with Accordion (In the
Theatre Box)**
*Le clown au bandonéon (A la
loge)*
1906
watercolour and pastel
78 × 46 cm
ex-Henri Simon Collection

29
**Woman at a Table (The
Procuress)**
*Fille accoudée (Minauderie,
ou L'Entremetteuse)*
1906
watercolour and pastel on card
30.8 × 24.1 cm
The Museum of Modern Art,
New York. Gift of Mrs Lillie P.
Bliss

30 (Plate 13)
Girl at the Mirror
Fille au miroir
1906
watercolour on card
72 × 55.5 cm
Musée national d'art moderne,
Centre Georges Pompidou,
Paris

31 (Plate 12)
Girl
Fille
1906
watercolour and pastel
71 × 55 cm
Musée d'art moderne de la
Ville de Paris

32
Circus Rider
L'Ecuyère (La Clownesse)
1906
watercolour and pastel
68.5 × 52 cm
Musée d'art moderne de la
Ville de Paris

33
Nude with raised arms (sketch)
Nu aux bras levés (esquisse)
1906
watercolour, pastel, chinese
ink and oil
54.4 × 35 cm
Musée d'art moderne de la
Ville de Paris

34
Old District (Costermongers)
*Vieux faubourg (Marchandes
des quatre saisons)*
1906
gouache
28.5 × 24.5 cm
Private Collection

35 (not exhibited)
Circus Performer
Fille de cirque
1906
watercolour and pastel on
paper
75 × 60 cm
Private Collection

36
**On the River (Landscape with
a Boat on the River)**
*Sur la rivière (Paysage avec
barque sur l'eau)*
1906
gouache
36 × 47 cm
Musée d'art moderne,
Villeneuve d'Ascq. Geneviève
and Jean Masurel Bequest

37
**Mother and Child (Mrs
Baignères and her son Jean)**
(sketch)
*Mère et enfant (Mme
Baignères et son fils Jean)
(esquisse)*
1906
watercolour
21 × 17 cm
Mrs John Hay Whitney

38
Dancer tying her laces
Danseuse laçant son soulier
1906
watercolour, pastel and
gouache on paper
21.5 × 25.5 cm
Kunsthaus Zurich. Dr Max
Bangerter Bequest

39
Female Head (sketch)
Tête de femme (esquisse)
c.1906
oil on paper glued on canvas
46 × 38 cm
Private Collection, Switzerland

40 (Plate 20)
The Accused
L'Accusé
1907
oil on card
74 × 103.5 cm
Private Collection

41
The Parade
La Parade
1907
watercolour and pastel
63 × 105 cm
Öffentliche Kunstsammlung
Basel, Kunstmuseum

42 (Plate 5)
Odalisque
Odalisque
1907
watercolour and pastel
63 × 97.5 cm
Öffentliche Kunstsammlung
Basel, Kunstmuseum

43
The Conjurer
L'Illusionniste
1907
oil and watercolour
44 × 33 cm
ex-Henri Simon Collection

44 (Plate 21)
The Bride (Aunt Sallys)
La mariée (Têtes à massacre)
1907
oil on canvas
74.9 × 105.4 cm
Tate Gallery, London.
Presented by the
Contemporary Art Society,
1935

45
Landscape
Paysage
1907
gouache on card
59 × 79 cm
Musée national d'art moderne,
Centre Georges Pompidou,
Paris

46
**Nude with raised Arms (Nude
doing up her hair)**
*Nu aux bras levés (Nu se
coiffant)*
1907
watercolour, pastel, chinese
ink and oil
54.5 × 35 cm
Musée d'art moderne de la
Ville de Paris

47 (Plate 16)
The Parade
Parade
c.1907-10
watercolour and oil on paper
65 × 100 cm
Musée national d'art moderne,
Centre Georges Pompidou,
Paris. Gift of Mme Rouault
and her Children.
One of the works which the
artist kept for over thirty
years: they acted as forms of
self-criticism. He called them
'witness pieces'.

48
In Court
La Cour
1908
chinese ink, watercolour and
gouache on paper
30.5 × 19.8 cm
Private Collection

49
In Full Flight
En pleine envolée
1908
watercolour
19 × 31 cm
Private Collection

50
Woman with Small Dog
*Silhouette de femme au petit
chien*
1908
watercolour
27 × 21 cm
Private Collection

51 (Plate 23)
The Accused
L'Accusé
c.1908
oil
84 × 64 cm
Private Collection

52
The Speaker
Conférencier
1908-10
oil on watercolour
106 × 85 cm
Musée national d'art moderne,
Centre Georges Pompidou,
Paris. Gift of Mme Rouault
and her Children.
One of the works which the
artist kept for over thirty

years: they acted as forms of
self-criticism. He called them
'witness pieces'.

53 (Plate 7)
The Canal Boat
La Péniche
1909
gouache on paper
58 × 88 cm
Musée de Grenoble

54
Woman with Feathered Hat
Femme au chapeau à plumes
1909
ink and watercolour
27 × 22 cm
Private Collection

55
**The Crowd (The Public at the
Law Courts)**
*La Foule (Public au Palais de
Justice)*
1909
gouache
19.5 × 31 cm
Fondation G. Rouault

56 (Plate 22)
The Tribunal
Le Tribunal
1909
oil
70 × 107 cm
Private Collection

57
Nasty Experience
Mauvaise rencontre
1909
oil, tempera and ink on card
78 × 56 cm
Valentin Collection – S.P.

58 (Plate 14)
Girls
Filles
c.1909
oil
90 × 60 cm
Private Collection

59
The Runaways (Exodus)
Les Fugitifs (Exode)
1909-11
oil
14 × 23.5 cm
Fondation G. Rouault

60
**The Steps of the Park of
Versailles, The Terrace**
*L'Escalier du Parc de
Versailles, La Terrasse*
1910
watercolour
68 × 52 cm
Musée national d'art moderne,
Centre Georges Pompidou,
Paris

61
Punchinello
Polichinelle
c.1910
oil over watercolour
71 × 56 cm
Musée national d'art moderne,
Centre Georges Pompidou,
Paris. Gift of Mme Rouault
and her Children.
One of the works which the
artist kept for over thirty
years: they acted as forms of
self-criticism. He called them
'witness pieces'.

62 (fig.i, p.31)
Bathers (composition)
Baigneuses (composition)
c.1910
oil
45.5 × 63.5 cm
Idemitsu Museum of Arts,
Tokyo

63 (Plate 26)
Hortense (sketch)
1910-19
watercolour and chinese ink
30 × 18 cm
Musée d'art moderne de la
Ville de Paris

64
La Belle Hélène (sketch)
1910-19
chinese ink wash, tempera and
pastel
31 × 19 cm
Musée d'art moderne de la
Ville de Paris

65
Winter (Poor Village)
Hiver (Pauvre village)
1910-19
gouache
39 × 47 cm
Private Collection

66
The Tragedian
Le Tragédien
1911
chalk, watercolour, gouache
and oil
39.7 × 29.9 cm
Private Collection

67 (fig.h, p.29)
Vale of Toil and Suffering
*Faubourg des longues peines
(Mère et enfants)*
1911
tempera, chinese ink and
charcoal
31 × 19.8 cm
Musée d'art moderne de la
Ville de Paris

68
The Baptism of Christ
Le Baptême du Christ
1911
watercolour, ink, gouache and
pastel
diameter 31.5 cm
Fondation G. Rouault

69
The Runaways (Exodus)
Les Fugitifs (L'Exode)
1911
gouache and chalk on card
45 × 61 cm
Kunsthaus Zurich

70 (Front cover)
Self-portrait as Clown
Pierrot blanc
1911
gouache and pastel on paper
80 × 65 cm
Private Collection

71
The Dwellings of the Poor
Les Demeures des miséreux
1912
mixed media on paper
28.8 × 17.1 cm
Private Collection

72
Maternity (Old District)
Maternité (Vieux faubourg)
1912
watercolour, pastel and
tempera
29 × 18.3 cm
Musée d'art moderne de la
Ville de Paris

73
Nude standing and Nude bending down
Nu debout et nu incliné
1912
oil
66.5 × 111 cm
Kunstmuseum Solothurn,
Josef Müller Foundation

74 (Plate 31)
Christ Mocked
Christ aux Outrages
c. 1912
oil
100 × 61 cm
Private Collection

75
Breton landscape
Paysage de Bretagne
c. 1912
tempera
54.5 × 72 cm
Private Collection, Switzerland

76
Woman at the Table
Femme accoudée
c. 1912
gouache on paper
30.7 × 19.2 cm
Private Collection

77 (Plate 25)
Beastly Rosa
Rosa la Rosse
1913
tempera with gum
43 × 30 cm
Private Collection

78
The Three Judges
Trois juges
1913
gouache and oil on card
75.9 × 105.7 cm
The Museum of Modern Art,
New York. Sam A. Lewisohn
Bequest, 1952

79 (Plate 24)
Acrobat X
Acrobate X
1913
ink, gouache and oil on paper
104 × 73 cm
Musée national d'art moderne,
Centre Georges Pompidou,
Paris. Gift of Mme Agnès Le
Dantec-Rouault

80
On the Lakeside (Spring)
Au bord du lac (Printemps)
1913
thin oil and pastel
23 × 69 cm
Private Collection

80a
Landscape (The Skaters)
Paysage (Les Patineurs)
1913
oil
20 × 60.5 cm
Musée d'art moderne de la
Ville de Paris

81
Verlaine of the Streets
Le Verlaine du fauborg
1914
oil and tempera on card
75 × 51.2 cm
Galerie Jochen Rackey, Bonn

82
The Reformer
Réformateur
1915
tempera, chinese ink, pastel
and paint
30 × 18 cm
Musée d'art moderne de la
Ville de Paris

83
Christ among the Soldiers
Christ parmi les soldats
1915-18
oil
46 × 62 cm
Kunstmuseum Solothurn,
Dübi-Müller Foundation

84 (Plate 27)
Nude with Long Hair seen from behind
Nu de dos aux cheveux longs
1917
chinese ink and gouache on
paper
38.3 × 23.5 cm
Private Collection

85 (Plate 29)
Face to Face
Face à face
c. 1917
gouache and chinese ink
105 × 74 cm
Private Collection

86 (Plate 28)
Project for Ubu Colon
Projet pour Ubu colon
c. 1917
gouache, chinese ink and
pastel
74 × 104 cm
Private Collection

87
Malikoko, For Ubu
Malikoko, Pour Ubu
c. 1918
chinese ink wash and colour
wash
40.5 × 30 cm
Private Collection

88 (Plate 32)
Christ on the Cross
Christ en Croix
c. 1920
oil
65 × 50 cm
Private Collection

89
Christmas Scene
Paysage de Noël
c. 1920
gouache
48 × 67.5 cm
Galerie Yoshii, Tokyo

90 (Plate 2)
Vase
1907
earthenware decorated with
two female figures
54 × 42 cm
Musée national d'art moderne,
Centre Georges Pompidou,
Paris

91
Vase
n.d.
earthenware decorated with
two female figures
54 × 42 cm
Musée national d'art moderne,
Centre Georges Pompidou,
Paris

92
Tragic Clown
Tête de clown tragique
1907
ceramic plate
24.5 cm
Musée de Grenoble. Agutte-
Sembat Bequest, 1923

93 (Plate 4)
Nudes
Nus
1911
ceramic vase
H. 19.5 cm
Private Collection

94
Nude
Nu
n.d.
ceramic
25 × 11 × 20 cm
Musée de Grenoble. Agutte-
Sembat Bequest, 1923

Bibliography

PRINCIPAL WRITINGS BY GEORGES ROUAULT

Souvenirs intimes, Paris, 1926

Le Cirque de l'Etoile filante, Paris, 1943

Divertissement, Paris, 1943

Soliloques, Neuchâtel, 1944

Stella vespertina, Paris, 1947

Correspondance Rouault–Suarès, Paris, 1960; repr. Tokyo, 1971; London, 1983

Sur l'art et sur la vie, Paris, 1971; Turin, 1972

PRINCIPAL WORKS ILLUSTRATED BY GEORGES ROUAULT

G. Rouault, *Souvenirs intimes*, Paris, 1926

G. Rouault, *Paysages légendaires*, Paris, 1929

G. Rouault, *Petite banlieue*, Paris, 1929

M. Arland, *Les Carnets de Gilbert*, Paris, 1931

A. Vollard, *Les Réincarnations du Père Ubu*, Paris, 1932

G. Rouault, *Le Cirque de l'Etoile filante*, Paris, 1938

A. Suarès, *Passion*, Paris, 1939

G. Rouault, *Divertissement*, Paris, 1943

G. Rouault, *Soliloques*, Neuchâtel, 1944

G. Rouault, *Stella vespertina*, Paris, 1947

G. Rouault, *Miserere*, Paris, 1948

G. Rouault, *Les Fleurs du Mal*, Paris, 1966

G. Rouault, *Visages*, Paris, 1969

PRINCIPAL WORKS ON GEORGES ROUAULT

G. Charensol, *Georges Rouault, l'homme et l'œuvre*, Paris, 1926

L. Venturi, *Georges Rouault*, New York, 1940

G. Diehl, *Peintres d'aujourd'hui: les maîtres*, Paris, 1943

J. Maritain, *Georges Rouault*, New York, 1953

P. Courthion, *Georges Rouault*, Paris, 1962; Tokyo, 1962; Milan, 1964; New York, 1977; Cologne, 1980

G. Marchiori, *Georges Rouault*, Milan, 1965; Lausanne, 1965

W. George, G. Nouaille-Rouault, *L'Univers de Rouault*, Paris, 1971; New York, 1971; Cologne, 1971; London, 1971

F. Chapon, I. Rouault, *Rouault: L'œuvre gravé*, Monte Carlo, 1978; Tokyo, 1979

B. Dorival, *Rouault*, Paris, 1982; Näfels, 1983; Norwalk, 1984

D. Molinari, *Rouault*, Musée d'art moderne de la Ville de Paris, Paris (catalogue raisonné of works by Rouault in the collection of the museum), 1983

C. Benincasa, *G. Rouault*, Turin, 1988

B. Dorival, I. Rouault, *Rouault: L'œuvre peint*, catalogue raisonné, 2 vols, Monte Carlo, 1988; Tokyo, 1990

F. Hergott, *Rouault*, Paris, 1991; Barcelona, 1991

PRINCIPAL EXHIBITIONS

New York, 1945, *Georges Rouault*, The Museum of Modern Art, text by J. Thrall Soby and Carl. O. Schiewind

Paris, 1952, *Georges Rouault*, Musée national d'art moderne, Paris, text by Georges Salles and Lionello Venturi

Arts Council of Great Britain, 1966, *Georges Rouault*, Edinburgh Festival, Tate Gallery, London, text by John Russell

Paris, 1971, *Centenaire de Georges Rouault*, Musée national d'art moderne, Paris, text by Michel Hoog

Paris, 1978, *Georges Rouault*, Musée d'art moderne de la Ville de Paris, text by François Chapon

Paris, 1982, *Hommage à Georges Rouault*, Musée du Grand Palais, Salon d'Automne, Paris, text by Bernard Dorival

Cologne, 1983, *Georges Rouault*, Joseph Haubrich Kunsthalle, Cologne, text by R. Beck and S. Gohr

Paris, 1992, *Georges Rouault, Première période, 1903-1920*, Musée national d'art moderne, Centre Georges Pompidou, Paris, text by Fabrice Hergott and others

Friends of the Royal Academy

SPONSORS

Mr Brian Bailey
Air Marshal Sir Erik Bennett
Mr P. F. J. Bennett
Mrs J. Brice
Mr Jeremy Brown
Mrs Susan Burns
The Clarkson Jersey Charitable
   Trust
Mrs Elizabeth Corob
Mr and Mrs S. Fein
Mr J. G. Fogel
Miss C. Fox
Mr and Mrs R. Gapper
Mr and Mrs Michael Godbee
Lady Gosling
Mr Peter G. Goulandris
Lady Grant
Mr J. P. Jacobs
Mrs Sonya Jenkins
Mr Harold Joels
Mr J. Kirkman
Mr and Mrs N. S. Lersten
Dr Abraham Marcus
The Oakmoor Trust
Ocean Group P.L.C.
Mr William Plapinger
The Rufford Foundation
The Worshipful Company of
   Saddlers
Mr David M. Shalit
Mr Robin Symes
Sir Brian Wolfson

ASSOCIATE SPONSORS

Mr Richard B. Allen
Mr Richard Alston
Mr Ian F. C. Anstruther
Mrs Ann Appelbe
Mr John R. Asprey
Mr Edgar Astaire
Lady Attenborough
Mr J. M. Bartos
Mrs Olive Bell
Mr David Berman
Mrs Susan Besser
Mrs John Bibby
Mrs Linda Blackstone
Mrs C. W. T. Blackwell
Mr Peter Boizot
Mr C. T. Bowring (Charities Fund
   Ltd)
Mrs J. M. Bracegirdle
Mr G. Bradman
Mr John H. Brandler
Mr Cornelius Broere
Lady Brown
Mr P. J. Brown Jr
Mrs A. Cadbury
Mr and Mrs R. Cadbury
Mrs C. A. Cain
Mrs L. Cantor
Carroll Foundation
Mr E. V. Cass
Miss E. M. Cassin
Mr R. A. Cernis
Mr W. J. Chapman
Mr Michael Chowen
Mrs J. V. Clarke
Mrs D. Cohen
Ms E. D. Cohen

Mrs R. Cohen
Mr P. Collin
Mrs N. S. Conrad
Mr C. Cotton
Mrs J. Curbishley
Mrs Saeda H. Dalloul
Mr John Denham
Mr Richard Dobson
The Marquess of Douro
Mr Kenneth Edwards
Mrs K. W. Feesey MSc
Mrs B. D. Fenton
Dr Gert-Rudolph Flick
Mrs J. Francis
Mr Gregory H. French
Mr Graham Gauld
Mr Victor Gauntlett
Mr Robert Gavron
Mr Stephen A. Geiger
Lady Gibberd
Mrs E. J. Gillespie
Mr M. L. Goldhill
Mrs P. Goldsmith
Mr Gavin Graham
Lady Grant
Mrs J. Green
Mr R. Wallington Green
Mr R. W. Gregson-Brown
Mrs M. Greissman
Mrs O. Grogan
Mrs W. Grubman
Mr J. A. Hadjipateras
Mr Jonathan D. Harris
Mr Robert Harris
Mr Mogens Hauschildt
Miss Julia Hazandras
Mr M. Z. Hepker
Mr Malcolm Herring
Mrs K. S. Hill
Mr J. Hoare
Mr Reginald Hoe
Mr Charles Howard
Mrs A. Howitt
Mr John Hughes
Mr Christopher Hull
Mr Norman J. Hyams
Mr David Hyman
Mrs Manya Igel
Mr C. J. Ingram
Mr S. Isern-Feliu
Ms K. B. Isman
Mrs I. Jackson
Lady Jacobs
Mr and Mrs Jaqua
Dr and Mrs George John
Mrs A. Johnson
Mr I. E. Joye
Mrs G. Jungles-Winkler
Mr and Mrs S. D. Kahan
Mr Simon Karmel
Mr D. H. Killick
Mr P. W. Kininmonth
Mrs L. Kosta
Mrs E. Landau
Mrs J. H. Lavender
Mr and Mrs Thomas Leaver
Mr Ronald A. Lee
Mr Morris Leigh
Mr and Mrs J. R. A. Leighton
Mr and Mrs R. Leiman
Mr David Levinson
Mr Owen Luder
The Hon. Simon Marks
Mr and Mrs V. J. Marmion

Mr B. P. Marsh
Mr and Mrs J. B. H. Martin
Mr R. C. Martin
Mrs G. M. S. McIntosh
Mr Malcolm McIntyre
Mr Peter I. McMean
Mr J. Moores
Mrs A. Morgan
Mrs A. Morrison
Mrs A. K. Morton
Mr A. H. J. Muir
Mr David H. Nelson
Mrs E. M. Oppenheim-Sandelson
Mr Brian R. Oury
Mrs J. Palmer
Mr J. H. Pattisson
Mrs M. C. S. Philip
Mr Ralph Picken
Mr G. B. Pincus
Mrs J. Rich
Mr Clive and Mrs Sylvia Richards
Mrs J. R. Ritblat
Robinson Charitable Trust
Mr F. P. Robinson
Mr D. Rocklin
Mrs A. Rodman
Baron Elie de Rothschild
Mr and Mrs O. Roux
The Hon. Sir Stephen Runciman CH
Sir Robert Sainsbury
Mr G. Salmanowitz
Lady Samuel
Mrs Bernice Sandleson
Ms J. Sandeman-Allen
Ms L. Schiff
Mrs Bernard L. Schwartz
Mrs L. Schwartz
Shell UK Ltd
Mr Mark Shelmerdine
Mrs Heather Shemlit
Mrs P. Sheridan
Mr Mohamed Shourbaji
Mr R. J. Simmons
Mr John H. M. Sims
Dr and Mrs Leonard Slotover
Mr and Mrs R. Slotover
Mrs Smiley's Charity Trust
Mr James S. Smith
Spencer Wills Trust
Dr M. Stoppard
Mrs B. Stubbs
Mr Robin Symes
Mr J. A. Tackaberry
Mr N. D. Tarling
Mr G. C. A. Thom
Ms Britt Tidelius
Mrs Andrew Trollope
Mr A. J. Vines
Mr D. R. Walton Masters
Mr Neil Warren
Miss J. Waterous
Mrs C. Weldon
Mr Frank S. Wenstrom
Miss L. West Russell
Mr R. A. M. Whitaker
Mr J. Wickham
Wilde Sapte
Mr Colin C. Williams
Mrs I. Wolstenholme
Mr W. M. Wood
Mr R. M. Woodhouse
Mr David Young
Mr F. Zangrilli

J.P.Morgan
Morgan Stanley International
Nikko Europe PLC
Northern Telecom
The Peninsular and Oriental Steam
    Navigation Co
Reed International
The Reuter Foundation
Rothmans International PLC
Rothmans International Tobacco (UK) Limited
The RTZ Corporation PLC
Salomon Brothers Europe Limited
Santa Fe Exploration (U.K.) Limited
Silhouette Eyewear
Smith & Williamson
Southern Water PLC
St James's Place Capital PLC
The Daily Telegraph
Thorn EMI PLC
TI Group PLC
Unilever PLC

Corporate Associates

31 PLC
Allen & Overy
American Express Europe Ltd
The Arts Club
A T & T (UK) Ltd
Bankers Trust Company
Banque Paribas
Barclays Bank plc
Barlow Lyde & Gilbert
Belron International BV
BMP DDB Needham
BMW (GB) Ltd
The BOC Group
Booker PLC
Bovis Construction Ltd
Brixton Estate plc
Burmah Castrol plc
Cable and Wireless plc
Carlton Beck
Charterhouse plc
CJA (Management Recruitment Consultants)
    Limited
Clifford Chance
CME. KHBB Ltd
Coca-Cola Northwest Europe
Coopers & Lybrand
Courage Charitable Trust
Coutts & Co
The Dai Ichi Kangyo Bank Limited
Dalgleish & Co
The De La Rue Company plc
Denton Hall Burgin & Warrens
Dowty Group plc
Durrington Corporation Limited
Enterprise Oil plc
Esso UK plc
J.W.Falkner and Sons Ltd
Fina plc
Forte plc
Foreign & Colonial Management Ltd
Gartmore Investment Management Limited
General Accident PLC
The General Electric Company plc
Global Asset Management
Granada Group
Guardian Royal Exchange plc
Halecrest – Design and Build
Hay Management Consultants Ltd
H.J.Heinz Company Limited

IBM UK Ltd
Inchcape plc
S.C.Johnson
Kleinwort Benson Limited
Kodak Limited
Laing & Cruickshank
Lex Services plc
Linklaters and Paines
London Life Limited
Y.J.Lovell (Holdings) plc
John Lewis Partnership plc
London Weekend Television
Macfarlanes
Mars Electronics International
Martini & Rossi Ltd
The Mercers' Company
Motion Picture Enterprises Ltd
Nabarro Nathanson
National Power plc
NCR Ltd
NEC (UK) Ltd
The Nestlé Charitable Trust
Nihon Keizai Shimbun Europe Ltd
Occidental International Oil Inc
Ove Arup Partnership
Pearson plc
Pentagram Design Ltd
Pentland Group plc
The Post Office
The Rank Organisation plc
Reliance National Insurance Company (UK)
    Ltd
Robert Fleming & Co Limited
The Royal Bank of Scotland
Royal Insurance Holdings plc
Sainsbury's plc
Saurer Group Investments Limited
Save & Prosper Educational Trust
Schroder Investment Management Ltd
J.Henry Schroder Wagg & Co Limited
Sears PLC
Sedgwick Group plc
Slough Estates PLC
SmithKline Beecham
Sony (UK) Limited
Sotheby's
Stanhope Properties plc
Sun Life Assurance Society plc
Tate + Lyle plc
Taylor Joynson Garrett
Tomkins plc
Trafalgar House Construction Holdings Ltd
United Biscuits (UK) Ltd
S.G.Warburg Group plc
The Wellcome Foundation Ltd
Wood & Wood International Signs Ltd
Yamaichi International (Europe) Ltd

Sponsors of past exhibitions

The Council of the Royal Academy thanks
sponsors of past exhibitions for their support.
Sponsors of major exhibitions during the last
ten years have included the following:

ALITALIA
Italian Art in the 20th Century 1989

AMERICAN EXPRESS FOUNDATION
Masters of 17th-Century Dutch Genre Painting
1984
'Je suis le cahier': The Sketchbooks of Picasso
1986

ARTS COUNCIL OF GREAT BRITIAN
Allan Gwynne Jones 1983
The Hague School 1983
Peter Greenham 1985

BANQUE INDOSUEZ & W.I.CARR
Gauguin and The School of Pont-Aven: Prints
and Paintings 1989

BAT INDUSTRIES PLC
Murillo 1983
Paintings from the Royal Academy US Tour
1982/84. RA 1984

BBC RADIO ONE
The Pop Art Show 1991

BECK'S BIER
German Art in the 20th Century 1985

ROBERT BOSCH LIMITED
German Art in the 20th Century 1985

BOVIS CONSTRUCTION LTD
New Architecture 1986

BRITISH ALCAN ALUMINIUM
Sir Alfred Gilbert 1986

BRITISH GYPSUM LTD
New Architecture 1986

BRITISH PETROLEUM PLC
British Art in the 20th Century 1987

BT
Hokusai 1991

CANARY WHARF DEVELOPMENT CO
New Architecture 1986

THE CHASE MANHATTAN BANK
Cézanne: The Early Years 1988

THE DAI-ICHI KANGYO BANK, LIMITED
222nd Summer Exhibition 1990

DEUTSCHE BANK AG
German Art in the 20th Century 1985

DIGITAL EQUIPMENT CORPORATION
Monet in the '90s: The Series Paintings 1990

THE ECONOMIST
Inigo Jones Architect 1989

EDWARDIAN HOTELS
The Edwardians and After:
Paintings and Sculpture from the Royal
Academy's Collection, 1900-1950 1990

ELECTRICTY COUNCIL
New Architecture 1986

ELF
Alfred Sisley 1992

ESSO PETROLEUM COMPANY LTD
220th Summer Exhibition 1988

FIAT
Italian Art in the 20th Century 1989

FINANCIAL TIMES
Inigo Jones Architect 1989

FIRST NATIONAL BANK OF CHICAGO
Chagall 1985

FONDATION ELF
Alfred Sisley 1992

FORD MOTOR COMPANY LIMITED
The Fauve Landscape: Matisse, Derain, Braque
and their Circle 1991

FRIENDS OF THE ROYAL ACADEMY
Elizabeth Blackadder 1982
Carel Weight 1982
Allan Gwynne Jones 1983
Peter Greenham 1985
Sir Alfred Gilbert 1986

GAMLESTADEN
Royal Treasures of Sweden, 1550-1700 1989

JOSEPH GARTNER
New Architecture 1986

J. PAUL GETTY JR CHARITABLE TRUST
The Age of Chivalry 1987

GLAXO HOLDINGS PLC
From Byzantium to El Greco 1987
Great Impressionists and other Master
Paintings from the Emil G. Bührle Collection,
Zurich 1991

GUINNESS PLC
Twentieth-Century Modern Masters: The
Jacques and Natasha Gelman Collection 1990
223rd Summer Exhibition 1991
224th Summer Exhibition 1992

GUINNESS PEAT AVIATION
Alexander Calder 1992

THE HENRY MOORE FOUNDATION
Henry Moore 1988
Alexander Calder 1992

HOECHST (UK) LTD
German Art in the 20th Century 1985

IBM UNITED KINGDOM LIMITED
215th Summer Exhibition 1983

THE INDEPENDENT
The Art of Photography 1839-1989 1989
The Pop Art Show 1991

THE INDUSTRIAL BANK OF JAPAN
Hokusai 1991

INTERCRAFT DESIGNS LIMITED
Inigo Jones Architect 1989

JOANNOU & PARASKEVAIDES (OVERSEAS) LTD
From Byzantium to El Greco 1987

THE KLEINWORT BENSON GROUP
Inigo Jones Architect 1989

LLOYDS BANK
The Age of Chivalry 1987

LOGICA
The Art of Photography, 1939-1989 1989

LUFTHANSA
German Art in the 20th Century 1985

THE MAIL ON SUNDAY
Royal Academy Summer Season 1992

MARTINI & ROSSI LTD
The Great Age of British Watercolours 1750-
1880 1993

MELITTA
German Art in the 20th Century 1985

PAUL MELLON KBE
The Great Age of British Watercolours 1750-
1880 1993

MERCEDES-BENZ
German Art in the 20th Century 1985

MERCURY COMMUNICATIONS
The Pop Art Show 1991

MIDLAND BANK PLC
The Art of Photography, 1939-1989 1989

MITSUBISHI ESTATE COMPANY UK LIMITED
Sir Christopher Wren and the Making of
St Paul's 1991

MOBIL
Modern Masters from the Thyssen-Bornemisza
Collection 1984
From Byzantium to El Greco 1987

NATIONAL WESTMINSTER BANK
Reynolds 1986

OLIVETTI
The Cimabue Crucifix 1983
Andrea Mantegna 1992

OTIS ELEVATORS
New Architecture 1986

PARK TOWER REALTY CORPORATION
Sir Christopher Wren and the Making of
St Paul's 1991

PEARSON PLC
Eduardo Paolozzi Underground 1986

PILKINGTON GLASS
New Architecture 1986

REDAB (UK) LTD
Wisdom and Compassion: The Sacred Art of
Tibet 1992

REED INTERNATIONAL PLC
Toulouse-Lautrec: The Graphic Works 1988
Sir Christopher Wren and the Making of
St Paul's 1991

REPUBLIC NATIONAL BANK OF NEW YORK
Sickert: Paintings 1992

ARTHUR M. SACKLER FOUNDATION
Jewel of the Ancients 1987

SALOMON BROTHERS
Henry Moore 1988

SEA CONTAINERS & VENICE SIMPLON-ORIENT
EXPRESS
The Genius of Venice 1983

SIEMENS
German Art in the 20th Century 1985

SILHOUETTE EYEWEAR
Egon Schiele and his Contemporaries from the
Leopold Collection, Vienna 1990
Wisdom and Compassion: The Sacred Art of
Tibet 1992

SPERO COMMUNICATIONS
The Schools Final Year Show 1992

SWAN HELLENIC
Edward Lear 1985

TEXACO
Selections from the Royal Academy's Private
Collection 1991

THE TIMES
Old Master Paintings from the Thyssen-
Bornemisza Collection 1988
Wisdom and Compassion: The Sacred Art of
Tibet 1992

TRAFALGAR HOUSE
Elisabeth Frink 1985

TRUSTHOUSE FORTE
Edward Lear 1985

UNILEVER
The Hague School 1983
Frans Hals 1990

VISTECH INTERNATIONAL LTD
Wisdom and Compassion: The Sacred Art of
Tibet 1992

WALKER BOOKS LIMITED
Edward Lear 1985

Other sponsors

*Sponsors of events, publications and other items
in the past two years:*
Academy Group Limited
Air Seychelles
American Airlines
Austrian Airlines
British Airways
Bulgari Jewellery
Cable & Wireless
Cathay Pacific
Champagne Bollinger
Christies International plc
Condé Nast Publications
Eileen Coyne
Dalena & Maccallini International Law Firm
Brenda Evans
Fina PLC
Forte
Hard Rock Café
Tim Harvey Design
Holiday Inn Worldwide
IBM United Kingdom Limited
Inter-Continental Hotels
Intercraft Designs Limited
Jaguar Cars Limited
A. T. Kearney Limited
The Leading Hotels of the World
Martini & Rossi
Merrill Lynch
Midland Bank PLC
Anton Mosimann
Patagonia
Penshurst Press Ltd
Polaroid (UK) Ltd
Princess Rama Malla
Ring & Brymer
Romilly Catering Co
Royal Mail International
Royal Nepal Airlines
Sherpa Expeditions
Paul and Mary Slawson
Mr and Mrs Daniel Unger
Kurt Unger
United Airlines
Venice Simplon-Orient Express
Vista Bay Club Seychelles
Vorwerk Carpets Limited
White Dove Press
Whyte & Mackay
Winsor & Newton
Mrs George Zakhem
Mrs Barry Ziff